The Berkeley Book

of College Essays

*Personal Statements for California Universities
and Other Selective Schools*

Third edition

Production by Evelyn Whitburn

Cover photo by Mark Coplan, Public Information Officer of the Berkeley Unified School District. The picture was taken at UC Berkeley's Greek Theater during Berkeley High School's 2004 graduation.

Janet Huseby is a freelance writer living in Berkeley, California. She began her career working with the Associated Press in Rio de Janeiro and has written for Time Magazine, Time Life Books, and the University of California, Berkeley. For the past seventeen years, she has worked with Berkeley High School seniors on their college essays.

Vicky Elliott, an editor and writer who has worked for the San Francisco Chronicle and International Herald Tribune, began reading college essays at Berkeley High when her older daughter applied for college in 2004.

Elaine Ratner has worked with Berkeley High seniors for five years. She is editor of more than 40 books and author of numerous articles, two cookbooks, and The Feisty Woman's Breast Cancer Book.

Published by the Berkeley High School Development Group
BERKELEY HIGH SCHOOL
1980 Allston Way
Berkeley, California 94704

All profits from the sale of this book will go to the Berkeley High School Development Group to support the school's College and Career Center.

The first edition of this book was published in 2006 by the Berkeley High Development Group under the title True Admissions. The second edition was published in 2007 by Stone Bridge Press as a Cody's Book under the title The Berkeley Book of College Essays.

ISBN 978-0-615-80798-0

Contents

Getting Started

FOREWORD

Most of the 700 or so seniors at Berkeley High School pass through my door during their senior year. As I get to know them and read their essays, I am often saddened to think that the only audience for their revealing and often heart-warming stories is the admissions committees of colleges around the country. I was very pleased when Janet Huseby proposed publishing a sampling of their essays, because then others would be able to share in the insights and reflections of this thoughtful, diverse group of teenagers.

As you will see from their stories, some live on their own, while others come from well-off families. Some take the bus to school, dropping off brothers and sisters on their way, while their fellow students are driven in SUVs. Some do not have computer or Internet access at home, while the student sitting in the desk next to them meets with a private tutor after school. Yet all are on their way to college, and their stories are compelling. Talking with students as they struggle to find the words to explain to the college admissions committees what makes them who they are, I realized that the college admission process in the United States has become like the rites of passage of previous generations all over the world. For these teenagers, this is a time to reflect on younger years and ponder the future, to sum up important questions such as, "Who am I in the world? How did I get where I am today? What goals do I have for the future? How is my identity defined by what I have done?" As part of the process, they complete numerous applications requiring them to fill in their name, address and Social Security number again and again. Students face up to their grades, reflecting on the work they have done for the previous three years, and make lists of their activities both in and out of school, often thinking about what they've accomplished and what they wish they had done. But it is the college essay that frequently is the most difficult for students, because it is where they try to put on paper the essence of who they are—a difficult task for accomplished writers, let alone students in their late teens.

When I asked some of our alums a year or more after their high school graduation for permission to print their personal statement, many told me that they thought their essays were "terrible" or "awful." Yet to me they are a snapshot taken during the first semester of their senior year of their vision of who they are, what they have come through and their hopes for themselves and the world. In that way, they give me hope as well. They show that the vast majority of teenagers do not fit the stereotypes depicted on the evening news, but are caring and responsible young people looking to make a better world for themselves and for all of us.

I hope that this book will serve as an inspiration to parents who struggle with their students through the demanding time of applying to college. And to students, as you try to keep your heads above water during the first semester of your senior year, realize that you are not alone, that many others have passed this way before and have matured and grown by using this time to reflect on where they have been and where they want to go.

But I also realize this is a powerful collection, and not just for the next generation of college applicants and their families. It is a beautiful portrait of a diverse, contentious and delightful group of young people. We adults have put them in a world that is often harsh and cruel, but they have found a way to redeem themselves and us with their generosity, perseverance and heart.

Ilene Abrams, College Advisor, Berkeley High School, 2003-2009

A WORD ON THIS BOOK

If you are about to write a college essay, there is nothing more useful than first reading other students' essays. This book is a good place to start: a collection of personal essays for the University of California and other selective colleges written by seniors at Berkeley High School.

The school, which forms a backdrop for many of the essays, is one of a handful of truly diverse high schools in the United States. In 2013, Berkeley had more than 3,300 students: 36 percent of the students were white, 27 percent African American, 13 percent Chicano/Latino, 10 percent Asian American, 14 percent of mixed race. Approximately 30 percent of Berkeley High students qualified for free or reduced lunch. Ninety three percent of the graduating class of 2012 planned to attend college.

I know Berkeley High well because I have spent the last 17 college application seasons—from September to the middle of December—sitting in the school's College and Career Center from 11:30 a.m. to 12:15 p.m. I am one of roughly fifteen professional writers, journalists, private counselors, and lawyers who annually volunteer to work with seniors on their personal statements on a drop-in basis—first come, first served, before school, at lunch, and after school. The College Center is a large, beautiful room with wide wooden tables and college banners tacked on the walls. When the bell rings, the room is wired. Students hustle in to be first in line to talk to the two college advisors about deadlines, recommendations, testing, transcripts. At the essay reader table, students start a makeshift wait-list, grab chairs, and wait their turn for editing and feedback.

I am a writer by trade, with a background in journalism. I started my career at the Brazil Herald, as a copy editor writing headlines and proofing the stock quotes. Then I landed a job at the Rio de Janeiro office of the Associated Press, trotting from a bombing of the Lan Chile Airlines offices to Great Train Robber Ronald Biggs' birthday party. By the time I had children, I was free-lancing in San Francisco. When my second daughter was writing her college essays, I realized that helping kids with their applications was something I could do. I offered my help to Rory Bled, who was then the Berkeley High college advisor. Next, I took on the task of organizing the volunteers who faithfully show up for the ten hectic weeks that comprise the main college application season, coaching students one by one through the most challenging of assignments, the personal essay.

The season starts in late September with the Early Admission and Early Action applications. At first, it is almost all girls who show up, focused and on task. In October, we start to see many more boys. The last minute is almost all male. Most students start out with a "telling" essay, a flat outline. "Show," we tell them. Why? Where? When? Explain. Describe. Once the details are there, throw out the introduction, scratch the conclusion—if you have told your story convincingly, they are wasted words. The advice is generic, but the goal is a story "only you can tell."

I have learned that essay reading is not so much about the English language as it is about marketing. Here's one essay that wasn't selling: It was about a best friend who was more popular, made better grades, and beat our essay writer out of a place on the varsity crew team. "I don't know about this," I said. "The colleges are going to want your best friend, not you." Then I found out the rest of the story. The best friend had quit the team and, in the following year, our writer was elected captain. The best part had been left out. "Put that in," I said. Another story: A student dropped out of a competitive sports team and was abandoned by all the teammates she had thought were her close friends. She was devastated, and wrote that the lesson she had learned was not to trust people. "Ouch," I said, "a college doesn't want someone who won't trust anyone." Then we got the rest of the story. Our writer reconnected with her old middle-school friends, and together they began helping at a children's center, a volunteer program that she eventually led. The final draft ended with her sailing past the mean girls out of the gates of Berkeley High, in good company, triumphant.

I have worked with an average of seventy students a year, keeping track of their names on the back of a large manila envelope. Not a year has gone by that I haven't heard of the deaths of at least two parents. One year, I read of two mothers who had had strokes; another year there were two fathers who committed suicide. I've read essays by an emancipated 16-year-old living on her own in an apartment, and a girl who drew strength from being looked after by "a large church filled with people wearing beautiful big hats and sharp suits." I've read essays from kids who are gay and from kids who struggle with poverty, taking care of younger siblings and translating for their parents. I loved an essay by one student who was the first in her family aiming for college. She compared taking Advanced Placement classes to visiting a foreign country. First, she explained, "I needed my passport, which was my transcript. Next, I needed to learn a new language." Her essay is in this collection. I liked the essay by the student who started out with a sports essay—a generic "no-no" of a topic—and then she surprised me by throwing in the theater! And I am fond of the student who laid her cards on the table without guile. "When asked to describe myself, I come up with words like 'cheerful,' 'creative,' and 'reliable,'" she writes. "But there is one adjective I usually try to push to the back of my mind in the hope that it will disappear: 'shy.'"

As essay readers, we tell kids there are a couple of basic things to avoid and rules to abide by. Don't preach; don't try to convert; describing hardship works if it ends in redemption; don't feel sorry for yourself, and don't ever complain—especially about having to help your mother, as one boy had the bad grace to do. Don't write about elementary school or even middle school. Watch out for sports essays and travel abroad and camp essays—good ones are hard to write.

One of the tricks college counselors use to help students who are having a hard time figuring out what to write is suggesting that they jot down a series of chapter titles of their life story and then expand on one of them. For the last seventeen years, I have finished every college admission season inspired by the idea of the personal essay and determined to write one of my own. I even have my list of chapters: "On the Boat to Brazil, or My Father the Engineer," "Barnard Blues," "Cub Reporter," and finally, "Sitting by the Sandbox." But, the fact is, I never do finish my own essay, perhaps because writing an essay in 600 words is hard work. I wish the students embarking on the challenge the best of luck.

Janet Huseby

APPLYING TO THE UNIVERSITY OF CALIFORNIA

University of California applications are due at the end of November. Currently, the UC application asks students to write two essays, using a maximum of 1,000 words in total. The essays may be of equal length, or one may be long and the other shorter. If you decide to write a long and a short essay, the university suggests that your shorter answer be no less than 250 words. The official prompts are as follows:

1. Describe the world you come from—for example, your family, community or school—and tell us how your world has shaped your dreams and aspirations.

2. Tell us about a personal quality, talent, accomplishment, contribution or experience that is important to you. What about this quality or accomplishment makes you proud, and how does it relate to the person you are?

The UC system does not ask for recommendations from counselors or teachers. Students are admitted on the basis of their high school classes and grades, test scores, a short list of extracurricular activities, and 1,000 words of their own. The lack of accompanying recommendations gives these essays a special burden. Unlike Common Application essays, UC essays must do more than give the reader a glimpse, however illuminating, into the writer's life.

The 1,000 words must cover: challenges overcome, passions, summers, family background, and a fleshing out of some activities outside the classroom. In the end, with 1,000 words complete, applicants should ask: Is this me? Is this everything that is important about me? Have I left anything out? You should also hand the essays to someone who doesn't know you, not a teacher or a counselor or a good friend—but someone who, like the college admission officer, is a stranger. Ask your reader to come up with some adjectives to describe you based on your essay. If the essays work, they will come up with a pleasing list. If you don't like the adjectives, it's time to rewrite.

Complete UC Essay Packages

This collection contains six complete sets of UC essays written between 2003 and the fall of 2012. Over the years, the University of California has consistently required applicants to submit a total of 1,000 words, but the format has varied. Before 2000, students were given three prompts and asked to write an essay on one of them. Between 2001 and 2006, applicants were told to respond to three questions. Now they are being asked to answer two prompts. While the format has changed through the years, the task has remained the same: Tell as much about yourself as you can in 1,000 words.

While not every student in the section below elected to attend a UC campus, they were all admitted to one or more.

ALBORZ YAZDI (class of 2013) was admitted to the University of California, Los Angeles, and UC Berkeley. He accepted an offer from Yale University.

1. The monitor before me displayed the outline of my best friend's skull and brain. He was in an MRI scanner, and I was in the control room outside with my supervisor, monitoring his brain activity as he looked at a series of pictures. We were comparing his neural responses to those of partially blind patients.

For one month this summer, I worked with a University of Pennsylvania research team at the Children's Hospital of Philadelphia, analyzing f-MRI scans for a study on patients with a rare degenerative eye disease called Leber's congenital amaurosis, or LCA. Ironically, these patients, who were so unfortunate as to slowly lose vision from birth, were lucky enough to have a form of LCA that gene therapy could cure. As I worked, I couldn't help but feel lucky to have my sight.

I began to think of other things I might have taken for granted. I was lucky enough to land a job at the University of Pennsylvania and co-author a scientific paper in high school. I was lucky enough to live in 2012, when safe flights across the country are only six hours long, and moreover, I was lucky enough to afford the flight. I felt lucky to have a piano in my house, lucky to have amenities like free speech and the right to protest, to be able to debate and write my opinions in the school paper. I felt lucky to use my body to play sports, rather than fight wars. I realized how lucky I was to have been saved by the marvels of modern medicine so many times, when I was on the verge of death from a lethal peanut allergy. Ultimately, I realized how lucky I was just to have been born.

My parents were not born into First World luxuries; they came to the United States from Iran in the 1980s, following the 1979 revolution. In Iran, as leftist students, they were persecuted. My mother, barred from university, came to study at UC Berkeley while my father was arrested and sentenced to death. His friends were executed one by one. After seven years on death row, he was released at the end of the Iran-Iraq war as a goodwill gesture and was able to escape Iran, reconvene with my mother in Europe, and to father me.

I have been granted my life and liberty. I realize, though, that I must pursue happiness: luck feels good, but it's not enough. The piano isn't going to play itself; nor will the paper write itself. There's more to life than luck. Luck is capital for me to take advantage of, but it's wasted without action.

In the same sense, I realized the MRI wouldn't run itself. Sure, our LCA patients were lucky to have a genetic defect small enough to be curable through gene therapy. But even this tiny gene wouldn't cure itself. Without my co-workers pioneering the technique, the patients would grow blind. Serendipity is only a part of the equation.

2. During a Speech and Debate tournament in my junior year, a judge handed me a word on a strip of paper: *cycle.* My task was to brainstorm for a few minutes and deliver a five-minute speech pertaining to the word.

I thought of bicycles, recycled garden compost, the Business Cycle; I searched my mind for anything of potential relevance. The judge then called time for me to begin. As I stood up to speak, I felt my heart beat faster. Of all the high school rites of passage, this moment was one for which I'd been eagerly waiting.

When I first enrolled in Berkeley High, I sought a playground for words: somewhere to build arguments as if building towers with Legos. I was surprised when I discovered that Berkeley High hadn't had a debate team since the 1980s. But I wasn't disheartened. I saw an opportunity to establish one. I took it.

Initially, when I announced I was creating a debate team, my friends in private schools with debate teams led by teachers and coaches, doubted me, as did school administrators. I kept my doubters in mind, as I struggled to write grants and solicit donations for computers and league dues, argued through bureaucracy, and foremost, looked for debaters at my school. The process was a macro-debate *per se*, on whether I could accomplish my goal.

"Cycle." I began to speak. Economic growth tends to cycle between boom and bust. I discussed the ups and downs of the technology and housing industries. I alluded to *Animal Farm*, and made an Orwellian declaration about cyclically oppressive governments: Oppression remained when Robespierre succeeded Louis XVI, when Stalin followed the Tsar, when Ayatollah Khomeini replaced the Shah.

I tried to assemble nuances of tone and inflection to make one moving sentiment, as if I were painting a work of art or composing a ballad. As I extemporized, I had an out-of-body experience. I heard my words turning ambiguous feelings into concrete convictions. I heard the way my brain interpreted "cycle."

When I finished my speech, I caught the gaze of my teammates from across the room, and we shared telepathic excitement. I recalled the first Speech and Debate meeting, how I couldn't convince my friends from water polo or lacrosse to stay, but did attract some other classmates to come practice competition rounds. A year before, we didn't think we'd be spending our Saturdays together, but here we were, happy that we'd created a network where any of the 3,300 Berkeley High students could practice argument, learning about the world and themselves.

Speech and Debate tournaments are about the exchange of ideas: knowledge, rhetoric, interpretation. For me, though, this tournament was about payoff. Although I didn't place first at that tournament, I did well. I found victory in Berkeley High's presence at the tournament, that Berkeley, home of the Free Speech Movement, had a public outlet for high school debate again. The cycle had gone full circle: I had revived Speech and Debate.

CARMELA ZAKON (class of 2004) graduated from Occidental College in Los Angeles in 2008, with a degree in critical theory and social justice. She has since lived in Brooklyn, New York, and Madrid, Spain, working as a policy researcher, tenant organizer, and English teacher. She was due to begin a master's program in urban planning in the fall of 2013.

1. From a young age, I learned to seek out resources to better myself. Being poor, I realize that no one is going to give me a handout. I have to go after my goals in order to improve my circumstances. It is with this mindset that I have pursued my educational aspirations.

My mom did not attend college, so I knew I did not have the

option of relying on her to inform me about preparation for college. I had to take the initiative to find a different method. In junior high school, I got involved with the Early Academic Outreach Program (EAOP) program. I was enthusiastic to be a member of a support system that could benefit me. I attended weekly meetings where we discussed the preparation necessary in order to become ready for further education. In high school, I became a member of Y-Scholars, another program that assists first-generation college-bound students. Towards the end of my sophomore year in high school, I received information about a program sponsored by EAOP, in conjunction with UC Berkeley, called the Pre-College Academy. As soon as I learned more about it, I had no doubt in my mind that I would be a part of the Academy. I went though the process of getting teacher recommendations and writing an essay. I was subsequently accepted into the program. I was willing to sacrifice a portion of my summer vacation and forgo wages from my job in order to take advantage of this opportunity.

As a student in the Pre-College Academy, I took courses in English Composition, Mathematics, and Psychology. I was enthusiastic—always participating in class discussion and putting a lot of effort into my work. I thrived in the University environment, where self-reliance and dedication is required. I went to my psychology professor's office hours when I wanted to know more about child development research. I met with the English Teacher's Assistant when I wanted advice to improve my essay on institutionalized power struggles. I had a personal drive to succeed, and had a great time doing it. My hard work paid off in the high quality of my performance, as well as in earning straight A's.

As a culmination of the program, there was a presentation of awards. When my name was called as the top student in the Academy, I was taken by surprise. This must be because I never worked for outside recognition: my desire to do my best had been my motivation.

Even though the grades I earned for these courses did not count for credit at my high school, I believe I gained a lot from this experience. I grew not only academically, but interpersonally as well. The self-confidence I developed made it possible for me to get involved in the YMCA's Youth and Government program when I returned to school in the fall. I became co-author of a mock education bill to set up inner-city students with one-on-one tutoring. This bill was the mock Governor's favorite of our Model Legislature and Court in the State Capitol.

In addition to Youth and Government, this past summer I was a participant in the Summer Law Institute at the UCLA campus. During this weeklong program, I attended lectures of law professors, defended in a mock trial, and met with law students and practicing attorneys. I have come out from each of these experiences stronger and more enthusiastic about continuing to explore my educational aspirations.

2. Being first-generation college-bound gives me a unique outlook and enables me to teach others. In addition, the fact that I am African American and come from a modest upbringing gives me a different perspective from many of my classmates. When we have class discussions, I am able to see situations from a different viewpoint from my peers and voice my opinions. For example, during a discussion in English the other day, a student made the comment that "We all come from middle-class homes." I was quick to raise my hand and offer a different perspective. Unlike my classmate, I know what it is like to not have enough food for dinner, to live in a crowded one-room apartment with my Mom and two sisters, and to have the phone service cut off due to unpaid bills. I feel privileged to be able to offer a different perspective on issues that many of the other students cannot relate to. This strengthens the class discussions because students can view arguments through various lenses. I feel most rewarded when I am able to witness my peers changing their perspective just a bit and say, "I never looked at it that way before."

3. My employment positions have helped me develop as a person. At age 14, I began my first job at the Berkeley Unified School District office, through the city of Berkeley Youth Works. I had watched my older sisters attain jobs before me, and I was pleased that it was finally my chance to earn a paycheck.

My duties at the work site consisted of typing, filing, phone operation, and in-person customer service. When I first began, I was somewhat apprehensive about talking to customers and helping them with their concerns. However, as time went by, I found myself beginning to enjoy helping others. I gained confidence in my abilities because I knew that other people were relying on me to do a good job.

Since then, I have moved on to other employment positions at Vista Community College and am currently working at a doctor's office. In each situation, I have taken the knowledge I gained from my first job and added to my skills. As an employee, I have not been able to participate in as many extracurricular activities as I would have liked, but I know that I have made good use of my time.

ELIZABETH CHO (class of 2013) planned to attend the University of California, Berkeley.

1. For the past seven years, I have lived in the heart of West Oakland, a city with one of the highest crime rates in the Bay Area and 32 percent of its population living below the federal poverty line. On the street corners in front of the liquor stores, I see brothers during the day and prostitutes during the night. Only 5 percent of the high school students in my neighborhood are eligible to apply to the University of California, and 12 percent are college-bound. West Oakland is neither the safest nor the nicest

neighborhood to live in; my parents thought differently.

My parents, first-generation immigrants from South Korea, chose to live in West Oakland. In the beginning, they had experienced many hardships, including the language barrier, financial difficulties, and cultural shock. Because they were not able to withstand these numerous hardships with their own ability, they received government benefits. Now successful, they wanted to support the community that helped them be where they are now. They thought of things they could do and decided to live in West Oakland and influence the community by living in it. My dad is a pastor and established his own Korean church, just five minutes away from my house. Through my dad's church, we bought a fourplex. We call it our *gong-dong-chae*, a faith-based community living. Here I live with my family of five, and the remaining two houses include one for single women and one for single men.

Inside the gates of our *gong-dong-chae*, we provide a small Korean community for our church members, mostly students abroad from Korea, to help them overcome the same hardships my parents went through. Being fluent in Korean, I instructed a conversational English class to help them be more comfortable when speaking English. When they have financial difficulties, we give them a lower rent. On Wednesdays and Fridays, we have traditional Korean dinners together. By providing a place where everyone speaks Korean and eats Korean food, my family helps them overcome any cultural shock they have.

Outside the gates, we do various types of outreach for our neighboring community. We pick up litter on the sidewalk in front of our house every day. We have prayer walks once a month, where we walk to various parts of West Oakland to pray and pick up litter. On Sundays, I take four people from my *gong-dong-chae* to the Open Door Mission to prepare hash browns, eggs, sausages, and cream of wheat for sixty homeless people in Oakland.

As I ride the 88, the public bus that takes me from Berkeley to West

Oakland, I notice the apparent differences in the communities; the landscape changes from organic cafes and recycling bins to street altars commemorating the murdered and litter on the sidewalks. Sometimes I wonder why I am living in this neighborhood, where it is too dangerous to take a jog around the block. But living here has given me a new point of view that I wouldn't have been able to see if I did not live here. Every day, I see the struggles that people go through. It reminds and compels me to be the social agent of change that will ameliorate my community. In eighth grade, I thought of ways I could help my community and began volunteering at the Open Door Mission. As I graduated from Willard Middle School and began attending Berkeley High, I began volunteering for Reading Buddies, a program that helps kindergartners at Washington Elementary School improve their literacy skills. During sophomore year, I began tutoring for the Young People's Program (YPP), which tutors and mentors eighth-graders in danger of not graduating at Willard Middle School. At YPP, there was an immense range in the students' academic ability. One student who wanted to become a professional football player struggled with basic multiplication and division. Because he knew that he was not good at math, he avoided doing math homework and instead acted defiant and told us he had no homework. Another student did not at all struggle with his academics; he was just too lazy to do it. But with enough support, they were able to graduate from eighth grade and successfully go onto high school. As a leader in all of these activities, I was able to urge my friends to volunteer and better the community.

Even though living here was not the most pleasant experience, I am going to miss the people, the fried chicken from the liquor store, and the graffitied taqueria. This neighborhood has become more than an outreach mission, it has become my neighborhood. In the future, I want to return as a doctor and improve the community that helped shaped who I am.

2. I never imagined myself playing field hockey and rugby. As a freshman, I was hesitant to start them. With only the bit of experience I had with floor hockey in elementary school, I was intimidated to try out for the team. The rule of using only one side of the stick was uncomfortable for me, but soon, dribbling up and down the field became second nature. For rugby, the rough culture itself was a worry for me as well as my parents. Even though tackling in the pouring rain leads to face plants in the mud, I get back up and do it again.

These sports aren't popular, let alone among women or Asians. But now, as captain of both teams, I am able to help new teammates with the same hesitations I had. I am able to encourage them in a discouraging game and push them to do their best whether in sprints or in a scrimmage. I learned how to be a leader, someone who makes my teammates into better players. Although sometimes even I am uncertain of going to tackle a girl three times my size, I tighten my core and go for the hit. Because as coach has always said, "Big trees fall hard."

GILLIAN SANDANHA (class of 2013)
planned to attend UCLA.

1. My school has a small cafeteria hidden among its many hallways. This room, home to the club "Best Buddies," is the place where I learned the true meaning of diversity.

Best Buddies International is an organization that fosters one-to-one friendships between mainstream students and those with intellectual and developmental disabilities. I was drawn to the cause in my sophomore year because I noticed that, despite the emphasis on diversity and accepting others at my school, many people had a blind spot when it came to people with disabilities. I remember sitting in my second period class, when a special needs student made an announcement over the school intercom. I was distracted by some classmates joking about "the retarded kid." Here was a brave student willing to address the entire 3,300 student body, being mocked for a disability over which he had no control. I had heard briefly about Best Buddies, but this incident pushed me to join the organization; to help people often overlooked. I am proud to say the student I heard on the intercom is my friend today, and that I am currently vice president of Best Buddies at Berkeley High School.

Despite my good intentions, I felt a little out of my comfort zone when I first stepped into the Special Education cafeteria. The first couple of weeks, I refrained from eating my lunch, feeling uncomfortable eating while watching others who could barely swallow their food. After a few more lunch meetings and conversations with the buddies, however, the place where I once felt slightly uneasy became one that I love.

Being in an environment such as Best Buddies exposed me to others' perspectives on life, and those assorted experiences have shaped who I am today. Towards the end of her senior year, my buddy Betsy, who has little function in her legs, would tell me how she practiced walking every day so she could walk the stage at graduation. "My parents are going to cry," she informed me. I would occasionally see her practicing walking in the hallway; her face focused as she carefully placed each foot in front of the other. It was inspiring to see Betsy work so hard for something most people take for granted. If Betsy could walk, I realized, practically anything is possible with determination, hard work, and some support.

A main aspect of Best Buddies is regarding those who may be limited physically or mentally as equals. Every week, we all come together and hang out. We've learned to work off each other and have fun. Betsy and I often draw together, since she prefers to stay indoors. Another girl in the club sings to her visually impaired buddy. Each pair finds something enjoyable to do, whether it's dancing, singing, or simply having a conversation. As I've learned, not everything works out. Often it's difficult to communicate with Betsy. Maybe it's easier to befriend some-one who is exactly like me, but my time with Betsy has been the most rewarding experience of my life.

2. I gaze out of the car window, mesmerized by the colorful saris and beautiful fabrics that characterize the streets of India. This happens each time I visit my family in Mumbai; it never ceases to amaze me how artfully the fabrics are designed and wrapped. My interest in fabric led me to take sewing lessons when I was in fifth grade. At my first lesson, I imagined I would soon be able to turn delicate fabrics into complex dress designs, with results as lovely as those I had seen in India. This, obviously, was not the case. I began with a plain cotton square and ini-tially sewed a very crooked line down the center. It took at least four lessons before that crooked line straightened out. Sewing did not come easily to me; it took many hours of practice before I could make some-thing even remotely close to what I had pictured that first day. I had to master what is so vital to sewing—patience.

As other sewing students came and went, I continued with sew-ing lessons for four years until I could sew independently. Those years were filled with many successes and a few mishaps. I once surprised my dad with a pair of pajama pants that turned out to be double his size. Another time, I cut out the fabric for a shirt the wrong way. The result was a shirt that stretched lengthwise instead of across, which made it very uncomfortable to wear. The feeling of excitement when I got things right, however, made all those hours of work worthwhile. My favorite piece of clothing that I made was a shimmery Christmas dress with a voluminous circular flare skirt. Most importantly, I learned something new from each project, regardless of the outcome.

I began to creatively design my own projects. My Halloween cos-tumes, for example, were unique. Among these were a spider dress, a double-sided witch cape, and a bumblebee outfit. Hour after hour, planning for the costumes, I would walk down the aisles of the craft store, lost among the hundreds of patterns and alluring fabrics until I found the ones that best fit my ideas.

I returned to sewing lessons this summer. This time, however, I was the instructor, teaching kids ages 6-14 years what I had once learned. I too learned many tips and tricks about sewing that I had either never known or forgotten. I realized that learning is a lifelong pursuit—my sewing improved when I first began my lessons, when I practiced on my own, and when I taught others. I hope to apply this process of learning to my other interests, including my love of piano, my ability to paint, and above all, my fascination with science.

Lucien Kahn (class of 2007) graduated from Vassar College and is working in the development department at the Haas School of Business at UC Berkeley.

1. Huge rectangles of light pour through the tall windows of UC Berkeley's Pauley Ballroom. Tables numbered 1 to 100 are lined up in perfect rows throughout the hushed hall. Some have been deserted; at others, opponents still struggle as time clicks away. Staring at the white and black pieces on the board before me, I imagine a sequence of moves, as seconds fall on the electronic screen at the edge of my board. I calculate each move twice to make sure I see all of the possibilities. "There are as many possible chess positions as there are atoms in the universe," I remember my chess teacher Robert telling me.

Across from me, my opponent, an old man with thin white hair, intently watches the board as if the miniature armies had come to life. When I am finally satisfied with my analysis, I grasp the white bishop and slide it across the board along its diagonal. I tap the button on top of the clock, stopping my timer and starting his. We have been concentrating for over three hours, and his timer is counting down the final forty-five minutes.

My dad taught me to play chess when I was 6 years old, and I began taking lessons at school. Over the years, I started a chess club at my middle school, gave chess lessons, organized a tournament, and worked as a paid tournament director. At Berkeley High, I continued to play both on the school team and in adult tournaments. As I became more and more serious about playing chess, I got up early each morning and set a timer for fifteen minutes to study chess from Judit Polgar's collection of over 5,000 chess problems. I have also researched the history and development of chess from its origins in ancient India. Because of my interest in glass-blowing, I decided to make a chess set out of glass, designing scale drawings for each piece and spending a day in an artist's glass studio to create them. The game ranks up there with my two other favorite sports, baseball and crew. Chess is incredibly complex, but beautifully simple when played well.

The old man moves his knight and hits the clock. Quiet, intense concentration returns. I sharpen my focus on the board to see how his move has changed my options. More space on the kingside, and my bishops are far more active than his pieces. If I can maneuver my knight and bishop to put pressure on his castle, I can create an attack he cannot defend. My plan may not work, but it's worth a shot. I lift my knight to an intimidating black square near his castled king, and tap the clock.

To me, chess is not just a game, it is an art. When I study a master's game, I appreciate the strategic organization of the pieces and the economy of each move. Because there are so many options in chess, there are many opportunities to make a mistake. But I learned that mistakes are part of playing chess. "To become a chess master, you must win a thousand games," Robert taught me. "But more importantly, you must lose a thousand games." When I learned that my mistakes are opportunities to improve as a chess player, I wasn't afraid of losing. I've taken this philosophy into other aspects of my life, as well, such as rowing and academics. In chess and life, I have found that I can always learn from my mistakes, but I can't succeed unless I am willing to put my pieces on the board and take risks.

2. My mom, dad, pets, and I have lived in the same house for all 17 years of my life. I love our old house, even if it is simple and lacks a few appliances. My mom and I cook popcorn the old-fashioned, stovetop way because we have no microwave. When it is time to clear the table, I wipe scraps into the compost; we have no garbage disposal—my dad says they are bad for the environment. And the dishes must be washed by hand, because, to my friends' horror, we have no dishwasher. "How do you do it?" they ask me.

"Well, … soap," I tell them.

Our house does have one room that few others have. Downstairs, behind a sliding wooden door, is my dad's darkroom. I remember helping him develop photographs when I was in elementary school. Just before the image began to emerge, he told me to say "Abracadabra." I was convinced that the magic word made the picture appear. Now I know that the magic is not in the word, or even the chemistry. True magic is finding beauty through patience, skill, and hard work.

My parents have taught me that how people live is more important than what they own, that creating is better than consuming, and that magic can be found in discovery and exploration.

3. Someone once asked me what my guiding philosophy was. I didn't know what to say at first. I knew it would have to have alliteration, one of my favorite figures of speech, and be funny but meaningful.

The motto I came up with was: "Mayonnaise in Moderation." For me, "Mayonnaise in Moderation" sums up how I can be happy in life. "Life is just like a sandwich," I explain to my skeptical peers, "not enough mayo and it's too dry; too much and it falls apart."

"What does that even have to do with life?" a friend objects.

"Well, putting mayonnaise on the sandwich is like taking risks in life."

As a kid, I erred mostly on the safe side, spreading the thinnest layer of mayonnaise I could possibly apply. As I grew and matured, I found that if I took an extra risk here and there, rewards awaited my gamble. During winter break of my sophomore year, I took an opportunity I previously would have been too frightened to accept; I rowed out beyond the Golden Gate Bridge, alone, in a single scull. That day, the mayonnaise was thick and the sandwich was almost falling apart, battered by waves. But sometimes a sandwich like that tastes just right.

NICOLO CORREIA (class of 2013)
planned to attend UCLA.

1. I stare at a photograph of a man who is familiar, but he doesn't know me. I've just located my biological father on Facebook. As I stare at a static screen, his profile picture elicits a strange combination of fluttering excitement and apprehension in my chest.

Long before this virtual encounter, I connected with my donor through different means. Under my bed lies a mass of rumpled notebooks, my most prized possessions. Their meaning has changed through the years. The majority of them now hold beginnings of short stories and journalistic interviews; but, at one time, the box housed hundreds of small scribbled notes, a one-sided correspondence with this man that was never sent. Before I started school, fathers were irrelevant creatures to me.

However, once school started, I found myself surrounded by schoolmates with fathers and often had to defend my family and cultural practices. Not only did my hand-drawn family picture look like an advertisement for polygamy—my mothers holding my hand on the right, and my sister following suit on the left— but also, when I spoke of family reunions of chorizo and *arroz con pollo*, I was told to tell the truth. To peers, I was totally WASP-y. I stopped trying to explain my family. This is when I began writing my donor, asking him questions like if his skin was as light as mine. Clearly, he had given me a lighter complexion than the rest of my family. My notes became a space that allowed me to tell my story, where no one could question its suitability.

Since those first literary exercises, my passion for writing has only intensified. In eighth grade, I felt confident enough to share my work. I sent an essay to all my teachers supporting my decision to skip school and instead march in downtown San Francisco in support of gay marriage. Walking down the streets in a throng of thousands, I realized my story wasn't unique. Protesters came from many non-traditional families like mine; and, as we marched, I felt comfortable telling my story aloud. It was then I decided story-telling was vital.

With this conviction, I've driven myself to grow as a writer. Joining *The Jacket* newspaper, I've worked in the news section looking for stories others might overlook. I also work on telling my own story by writing short memoirs, recently having my first story, "Accidental Drag Queen," published online. In childhood, the written world was my place to escape, where I talked to my biological father and used my imagination. I no longer need to keep my work hidden under a bed. Scrolling back through the Facebook account, I realize I'm not so different from my donor. He, too, has an interest in writing, having majored in English and broadcast journalism. By agreement, I cannot contact him until I am 18. When I do, I plan to forward him a long-overdue letter, a thank you for fueling the beginnings of my writing career.

2. It's my first day on the job, and I am plunged into pandemonium. Opening the door to the studio, I find scripts scattered on desks, phones chirping, and people huddled around a television screen shouting directions for edits. This is not what I imagined when I secured an internship last summer with Sacred Land Film Project, a film company that chronicles the struggles of indigenous peoples.

I grew up believing the *30 Rock* myth of media production. In my head, the process of making films featured several wacky writers, actors, and corporate bosses getting into outlandish situations, seemingly doing no work, yet a popular variety show would emerge each week. At Sacred Land, there was no Tina Fey uttering one-liners, only a hub of activity. Right away, I knew that to prove myself I needed to get busy.

At my first weekly business meeting, I felt impossibly young. My coworkers, in their twenties and beyond, were furiously typing notes into their MacBooks and talking film jargon. Not one to back down from a challenge, during the next week I poured over Internet film sites and software, reviewing everything from types of film shots to scriptwriting programs like Celtx. I was learning a foreign language, and it paid off. The next meeting, I conversed fluently, expressing concern with timecode placement in scenes from *Standing on Sacred Ground*, the current documentary production, and jotted down notes for stock footage to research for it.

Now my duties include assisting a screenwriter. Taking the rough footage, I "conform" the script of our film. This entails editing many hours of interview footage and composing comprehensible scenes from the rough cut. This may sound simple enough, but when the script is written in an almost extinct language from Ethiopia's Gamo highlands, and cutting a sentence of dialogue can be an hours-long discussion, things get a tad more complicated. However, the work is well worth the effort of producing a crisp and intelligent scene. As part of the production team, I've learned a lot about scriptwriting. I've also had the honor to learn about and help present the struggles of the Gamo people. Art and activism, what more could I ask for?

Five months later—my internship grew into a yearlong commitment—I open the office door to the same chaotic scene. I'm no longer overwhelmed. I walk to my desk and begin work on my newest assignment, helping create a script for a two-minute fund-raising film. With it, we hope to raise $100,000 for film production costs. Sacred Land Film Project isn't *30 Rock*, but that's good. In combination with my film and writing classes, it is where I am turning my passion into accomplishment. With all this work, I'm not sleeping much, but I am happy.

Essays long and short, common and not ...

With a few exceptions, most private schools now use the Common Application, which as of 2013-2014 asks for one essay, of at least 250 words and no more than 650. However, many private schools round out the Common App with supplementary questions. Most students applying to private colleges and universities end up needing at least two long essays, along with several short-answer essays. California students often use one of their UC essays for the Common App and the other one for supplemental questions.

The Common Application questions for 2013-2014 were as follows:

- *Some students have a background or story that is so central to their identity that they believe their application would be incomplete without it. If this sounds like you, then please share your story.*

- *Recount an incident or time when you experienced failure. How did it affect you, and what lessons did you learn?*
- *Reflect on a time when you challenged a belief or idea. What prompted you to act? Would you make the same decision again?*
- *Describe a place or environment where you are perfectly content. What do you do or experience there, and why is it meaningful to you?*
- *Discuss an accomplishment or event, formal or informal, that marked your transition from childhood to adulthood within your culture, community, or family.*

Most of the following essays are either the Common App main essay or one of the UC essays. In the cases where the essay is responding to a supplementary question, I have included the question.

AARON MAZEL-GEE (class of 2005) graduated from Brown University in 2009 and is a visiting scholar at MIT, while working on a PhD in theoretical math at UC Berkeley.

With considerable curiosity, uncertainty, and apprehension, I decided to embark on a five-week "language and culture exchange" in China last summer. As one of thirty American students living at a Beijing university, I'd explore the history, language, and culture of a side of me I had thus far ignored.

I felt anxious about my decision to go to China. Having never closely connected with my Chinese heritage, I worried that I would scarcely belong. My experiences growing up were different from those of the few Chinese kids I'd known. As the child of a white Jewish mother and

Chinese father, I've come to recognize that growing up biracial is an enormous asset, but I didn't always feel this way.

For a long time, I found myself forced to straddle cultures, never able to call one country my ancestral homeland. There rarely were family gatherings of the sort my single-cultured friends enjoyed, where both sides—at least temporarily—become one. Not only are the two sides of my family separated by different customs and interests, they don't even share a common language.

At first, I sensed the need to choose one side or the other, as if they were baseball teams squaring off. To my father's disappointment, I connected much more with my mother's side. I went to a Jewish preschool and later to an extracurricular religious school, all of which culminated in my bar mitzvah. After that, I joined two Jewish high school programs.

Almost as an afterthought, I attended a Sunday Chinese school during third and fourth grades. I never made many friends there, however, and because of soccer practice, piano lessons, and religious school, Chinese school fell by the wayside. Almost all my friends were Jewish, and our common culture bound us. I never formed such lasting connections with Chinese friends or customs, besides the occasional Chinese New Year's family banquet or the money-filled red envelopes traditionally given by Chinese grandparents.

On the trip, however, I realized that I do belong. I identified with many more aspects of Chinese life than I had ever expected. Standing on the Great Wall, I could look back into history to see my ancestors building it. Watching Shaolin monks practice martial arts, I was reminded of the martial arts classes that comprised the "cultural" aspect of my Chinese school, one of my favorite parts. The food was similar to the food I ate at home, and the people looked similar to half of my extended family.

The greatest surprise, however, was that I fit in with the other students. Although I wasn't fully Chinese, I felt as much a part of the group as the others. We all shared a common tie—an interest in our heritage. No matter how we had been raised, we were all connected to this vast country and its history.

As a result of this special opportunity to submerge myself in Chinese culture, I feel liberated and more comfortable with my Chinese roots. I have deepened the connections with my Chinese relatives and no longer feel the need to shy away from that part of my background. The discussions of Chinese American identity that my father often encourages have taken on new meaning for me. Living in China has taught me how important it is to challenge myself in order to broaden my personality and sense of self.

ABIGAIL SMITH (class of 1994) graduated from Dartmouth College in 1998 and from Tuck Business School in 2005. Between college and business school, she returned to Berkeley High to teach math. She currently works as a consultant in the Bay Area.

"She's OUT!" I yell in my best umpire voice. I stand up slowly, stretching to my full five feet, one inch, daring anyone to question me. The game is over, Dr. Brennan's Smile Makers winning by a whopping 24 to 16.

I never feel more lonely than when I'm standing in the middle of a baseball diamond wearing my bright yellow umpire's jacket. Unlike the players, I do not have a coach, teammates, or parents on my side. It's my job to call the plays, keep track of the outs and make sure each girl gets enough playing time. I must make sure that the coaches are respecting the players, the parents are respecting the coaches, and that I'm conducting myself in such a way that everyone respects me. The league in which I'm an umpire is a girls' softball league for second- to fifth-graders. Its purpose is to teach the girls how to play softball, but more important, how to play on a team. What I've found most challenging, though, is dealing with parents and coaches who become impatient watching the game, which is full of bungled plays. They often take their frustration out on the umpire.

When I started umpiring three years ago, I had a hard time dealing with angry coaches and parents. Just as the players were learning to play softball, I was learning to be an umpire. As time went on, not only did I get to know the rules better, but I learned to hold my hands up and yell out, "Dead ball!" knowing that I was right. I learned to listen to the coaches when they complained and then to tell them, calmly, that my call would stand. I learned that when I did make a bad call, I had to put it behind me; I could not let myself get shaken up. I learned that looking straight into the coaches' eyes would make them realize that I couldn't be pushed around.

My favorite time is when a girl gets up to bat and just slams it, way out there. I love the sight of the coaches frantically waving the runners on and the teammates lining up to congratulate the usually astounded batter. As a graduate of the league, I remember the thrill I felt when I reached home plate. But I also remember watching the umpires and wanting to be one. In a girls' league, where most of the coaches are men, I feel that it is important for the girls to see me in a position of authority.

Because umpiring is such a lonely job, I've had to become my own coach and my own teammates. Just as the coaches tell their girls, "Good job out there," I always congratulate myself after a call. I have gotten some strange looks from players as I walk back to my favorite position between first and second, saying out loud, "Good call, ump, keep it up!"

Over the years, I have gained a reputation in the league. The coaches know that I'm fair, they know that I'm doing my best, and they know that I'm having fun. In my first year of umpiring, coaches contested my calls because they knew that with a little bullying, I would back down. They don't even try any more.

The game is over, the players are eating their snacks and the parents are picking up discarded mitts. I regretfully take off my yellow umpire jacket and return it to the head coach of Dr. Brennan's Smile Makers. He smiles at me and cheerfully signs my umpire payment card. Now I have to make the long trek across the diamond into the dugout of the losing team, Chez Panisse. Silence falls over the crowd as I present my payment card to be signed. The coach grimly takes my card and signs it. As I reach for it, he shakes my hand. Then, smiling, he says deliberately, "Good game, ump."

ALYSSA PACE (class of 2013) planned
to attend UC Santa Barbara.

Breakfast trays are empty before the last half of the campers have even made it through the Dining Hall doors. "Bacon!" I yell to the busy kitchen staff, throwing a tray in the exchange window. I tap my foot impatiently, scanning the D-Hall for more potential refills. Because the D-Hall department is over-capacitated and understaffed this week, I have been requested to volunteer in my ex-department before Kiddie Kamp opens. Sizzling bacon is handed back to me, and I make a beeline for Table 27. Just as I begin to congratulate myself for my expert maneuvering skills, I slip on a puddle of spilled orange juice, and the fresh tray of bacon flies through the air, crashing on the floor. Humiliation hits me in a wave, but my incident is barely noticed over the buzz of early morning chatter. I take a deep breath and collect my equilibrium; then I'm on the floor, scrambling to collect the bacon and wipe up the grease.

I spent my entire childhood waiting to become a staff member at

Tuolumne, a family camp in Yosemite. But even after two employed summers working three different department positions, camp is more challenging than I ever imagined as a camper. It's not only work; it's a lifestyle. Camp is handling stressful situations, developing reflexes, and accepting unexpected responsibilities. It's sharing an 8-foot by 10-foot room, living on Sysco food, and being away from home for ten weeks. It's learning, struggling, and tolerating. But more importantly, it has been the best experience of my life. Running an entire camp with only sixty other young adults has instilled newfound independence that allows me to demonstrate leadership skills in other areas of my life.

When I returned from my first summer of work, I confidently joined Berkeley High School leadership as a Student Site Council representative. In this position, I act as a voice for the student body by meeting weekly with our student leadership and biweekly with the School Site Council, a school policy-setting group that includes our principal, teachers, and parents. Because of my experience with family camp, I feel comfortable talking to and sharing my opinions with adults. Together, we have successfully improved the BHS counseling department, created a peer math tutoring program, and organized relief efforts for Hurricane Sandy. Within my 3,300-student school, as I did within my 60-member staff family, I have realized my impact—and truly believe in it.

After my shift in the D-Hall ends, I whip off my apron and dart to Kiddie Kamp, my current department, to start my usual work hours. I am greeted at the gate by a parent who asks, "You work in Dining Hall and Kiddie Kamp?" After explaining my situation, the parent shakes her head, smiling. "I don't know how you kids do it." I laugh with a shrug, then begin my morning shift.

ANDREW GORDON-KIRSCH graduated from UCLA
in 2010 and received a Dorot Fellowship to study in Jerusalem.
He now works for J Street in New York as a political organizer
specializing in Middle Eastern and Israeli/Palestinian issues.

As I cross the striped white lines on the sticky black pavement into enemy
territory, I look up with awe at the mansion in front of me. How could
such a fine resort lower itself to maltreating its employees by binding
them with a contract that underpays, doesn't provide affordable health
care, and denies them unionization? I shake my head with a sigh as I enter the Claremont Hotel through a side door, where they won't expect to
find lobbyists like me and my delegation of socially aware teenagers.

"Hi, my name is Andrew. I would like to speak with your manager."
I'm the entry man. I get us into the dark depths of administration.
The manager of room service tries to plead innocent, saying she has
no authority. A finance manager says it's her superiors that are making the bad decisions. Finally, we deliver our message to the restaurant
manager. Our tactful push for improved employee contracts receives
a canned response. "Thanks for your concern, I'll be happy to call my
boss and relay your message to him." Seeing right through his transparent lie, I bring out my cell phone, gesturing for him to take it from
my hand. He steps back with a quizzical look. "What are you doing?"
"My phone has unlimited weekend minutes," I say, "Feel free to make
that call right now." Of course, he refuses, and, in no time, we are being
herded through the main lobby, past the wedding procession, and out
the glass doors. Our group made such an impression—a tranquil one,
of course—that hotel security escorted us off the premises!

I was at the hotel with Jewish Youth for Community Action (JYCA),
a local program, student-created and led, which has educated and inspired political and cultural awareness in the community and in me.

We seek progressive social change through youth empowerment and through taking action in our community. We protest, picket, and lobby. We also give workshops on facilitation, community building, and pressing social issues like homelessness, abortion rights, and the Israel-Palestine conflict.

In addition to helping members of my extended community, I proactively aid members of my immediate community: students at my school. A new student at Berkeley High has it hard. Students from abroad have it three times as hard. Not only are they in a new environment, but the environment doesn't speak their language, nor does it practice the same customs. As chairman of Berkeley High's Ethnic Culture and Language Exchange, I work closely with newly arrived students in the English Learners Department (ELD) to make them feel more at home in the United States and at an American high school of 3,000 students. At least once every month, we pair native English speakers with ELD students in an exchange where both sides gain insight on the other's experiences. I facilitate interactive games such as multilingual telephone and "Simon Says." Outside of club meetings, I connect with ELD students by eating lunch with them and showing them around campus. Rodrigo, who had been in the United States for a week, had questions about English vocabulary—the pronunciations of *through, thorough, cough*, and similar words that end in *-ough*. Delia, from Colombia, wanted to know how government works in America. I tried my best to explain to her the divisions of power and the levels of federalism in simple terms. I made sure to add that America promotes public participation—it's in the Constitution—and that it's up to us activists to ensure that we are headed in the right direction.

She went for a walk and didn't come back. In one split second, a driver took my mom's life and shattered my family. And as I grappled with the horror of this terrifying reality, she wasn't there to comfort me. She was gone. As a 9-year-old, I had to figure out the pain on my own.

My dad had his own grief. He had lost his wife of twenty-three years, and with her went the life he had always known. He was devastated; unsure of how to pick up the pieces of our family. He didn't know how to deal with my pain, how to comfort a child who missed her mom. And he still doesn't.

After eight years as a single parent, he has yet to assume the fatherly role I long for him to take. Our interactions are superficial—he works, I go to school, he gets home, I do homework. We don't discuss the world or politics, or his life or mine. There's no mention of his job, my classes, or a funny story. If I'm frustrated, I can't talk to him about it. If I'm sad, he's not there to give me a hug. He works so hard to provide for us, but he can't provide the emotional support I need the most. So I take care of myself.

I buy the groceries so there's food in the refrigerator. I wash my clothes so they don't sit in the basket. I do the things I see my friends' parents do for them, like filling out school forms or obtaining a parking permit. My dad doesn't want any part of the family dinners that I so crave and want to recreate, so I cook for myself, or sometimes end up eating cold cereal in my room, accompanied by my physics book. I've learned that tears don't help. No matter how hard I try to make our relationship deeper, it doesn't change.

But what I can't get from my dad, I get from my friends, both young and old. My friends are always there for me and love me unconditionally. These are the people who support me when I've had a rough day and who are proud of me when I win a school election. They come to my dance performances and field hockey games, and they bring me soup when I'm sick. They are my true family, the one that my dad can't quite figure out how to create. With them, my life is rich, joyful, and meaningful.

My mom is gone, there's nothing I can do to change that. I've almost come to accept it. But I maintain hope for me and my dad. There's a chance we haven't lost it all. I'll be ready for the day when my dad decides to be the father I long for, but until then, I'll continue to develop independence and enjoy the rich relationship I have with my friends.

ANONYMOUS II

"In a world where change is inevitable and continuous, the need to achieve that change without violence is essential for survival."
—*Andrew Young, former mayor of Atlanta*

In my world, change is mostly inevitable only if violence follows its course.

When my sister's boyfriend, Ervin, was gunned down, everything inside me broke. I screamed and cried and looked at the door waiting for him to come. At the hospital, I took my sister in my arms and let her cry, and prayed to God. Ervin wanted a different life for himself, but his path to change included violence. He pushed people to the bottom by selling them crack cocaine.

The day he was murdered was when I started thinking about my own survival.

My nephew Maurice and I are like brother and sister. Growing up, he was my secret keeper and I was his; or at least I thought so. Last spring, Maurice tried to kill himself. He never shared any of his pain with me. All I could think about was why would the happiest person I know try to kill himself? Did he think that that was his only way out?

Everyone wants change without violence, but most people in my community don't know how to do it. Young people fall victim to their "role models" and "idols," who convince them that they won't be able to make money unless they get into the streets. It's hard to find hope. There is always someone saying that you can't make it.

Even before my mama was born, the odds were against her. The way she started coping, with relatives believing that she would not amount to anything, was drinking. Growing up, I watched every painful memory and stressful day be popped open and poured into a glass of destruction and burn down her throat to devastation and sorrow. And still I watched her get back up in the morning and keep pushing. Early on, I took on the responsibility to try and be my mama's hope.

Education has been my path to survive. My after-school activity was being at the Y, where I studied, determined to be knowledgeable so that I will have a way out.

I want to be the person who will empower African-American youth and help them believe that we can survive without destruction. I hope to become a successful therapist and set an example that we do not have to keep pulling each other down in order to survive.

ARI ROKEACH (class of 2007) attended UC Davis and is working in the client management department of a Bay Area financial management firm.

Among my teachers, I'm known as Ari Rokeach. But to my friends, I'm also known as *torriealba@yahoo.com*. This e-mail handle (albeit with a twist on the spelling) is a tribute to my favorite baseball player, Yorvit Torrealba, a former catcher for the San Francisco Giants who never re ceived the recognition he deserved. And it gives a clue about who I am: an avid player of fantasy sports who can spot talent a mile away.

My older cousin Josh introduced me to fantasy baseball one weekend when I was in ninth grade. He explained how each manager drafts a team of players from Major League Baseball, applying the players' real-life stats to the fantasy team as he competes against other managers in the league. The fantasy manager adds, drops, and trades players, scouting just as in real baseball. Mesmerized by his explanation, I promptly enrolled in his league.

But I didn't stop there. I took it upon myself to be a fantasy baseball ambassador, creating my own league and inviting nine of my friends to join along with my younger brother, Zach, who was still in junior high.

Fantasy baseball was unlike anything I had ever done before. Suddenly, I was the manager of my very own baseball team. Not only that, I was the commissioner of a league with ten teams under my influence. I determined which player stats would count, how many pitchers and hitters could be on each team's roster, and a nominal entry fee.

My fascination with fantasy baseball expanded into other sports as their seasons rolled around, first fantasy football, and then fantasy basketball. Now in my fourth year of fantasy sports—as both a team manager and a league commissioner—I've mastered the art of sniffing out up-and-coming players and measuring the worth of aging superstars. About a month before a draft, I begin to comb through the Yahoo and ESPN sites, reading experts' articles about various players' potential. Then, I cross-reference the projections with how the players have performed in past seasons to come up with my list of top picks for the draft.

When I started AP Statistics this fall, it was with a leg up: I already had exposure to real-world applications of statistical analysis. And, thanks to my daily dose of the San Francisco Chronicle's sports pages and the various sports news websites, I've picked up the lingo of sports writing. In the spring of my junior year, I decided to put that new language to work by writing a series of sports articles for Berkeley High's *Jacket* newspaper, graduating this fall to my own column dedicated to professional sports.

After herding my friends through all the complex steps of drafting and managing their fantasy teams, and mediating the many disputes that come with the league commissioner territory, the role of co-captain of the men's varsity water polo team at Berkeley High this fall came easily to me. I walked the line between drill sergeant and cheerleader, guiding fifteen brawny guys in grueling dry-land warm ups and helping to lead the varsity team to its first league championship title in five years.

Most importantly of all, fantasy sports have brought me closer to the people in my life, and especially to the person who sits a couple of feet away from me every night, my brother Zach. As we sit back-to-back while facing our computer screens and traveling through the virtual world of fantasy sports, we trade tips about players and bounce our planned trades off each other. The more we connect and bond over our shared passion, the more the age difference between us disappears.

ARIANNA TABOADA (class of 2006) graduated from UCLA in 2010. In 2012, she completed her master's in maternal/child health and social work at the University of North Carolina in Chapel Hill, and currently works as a consultant in the field of sexual and reproductive health.

As I stepped onto the stage, tightly gripping the microphone, I inhaled deeply and took my place at the small X marked in the middle of the stage. The curtain came up and without hesitation, I began to speak. "*Buenas noches, cómo están?*" The crowd cheered in response, and I quickly repeated myself in English, "Good evening, how is everyone doing tonight?" The response was equally deafening. I had emceed three years now for En Pointe Youth Dance Company. "For those of you who aren't familiar with En Pointe, we are a youth dance company from California, founded by two Berkeley teenagers when they were in the seventh grade." Well, no one was familiar with En Pointe in this town; we were in the middle of what is known as colonial Mexico.

I proceeded with my introduction, first in Spanish, then in English. "Everything, from lighting and sound, choreography and costumes, fund-raising, and, of course, dancing, is run by youth." My position with En Pointe had grown over the years, from usher, to emcee, to spokeswoman. My involvement grew each year, and this year, as we took on our latest artistic endeavor, I became the public relations manager. Honestly, this title doesn't accurately describe my role. I was simply helping carry out a dream that had been born a year earlier: bringing a group of Berkeley dancers to Mexico to participate in a dance and cultural exchange.

Like many first-generation Mexican Americans, I grew up in Berkeley speaking both Spanish and English. My parents attended higher education in the United States and fully understand and support the importance of both English fluency and maintenance of native language, but it is a challenge in American culture. My parents worked to enforce the rule of "English at school, Spanish at home." At the dinner table, it was Spanish only; if we asked for the bread to be passed, no one passed the basket until we asked in Spanish. Never having been enrolled in formal Spanish language classes, our vocabulary was limited in certain areas. There were times when my sisters and I began to speak in Spanglish to each other, which my parents absolutely forbade, fearing it would corrupt both our languages. We would have conversations about school, work, even boring things like computers, all in Spanish, in order to increase our vocabulary. It is a problem for many Mexican-origin families to squeeze Spanish into an

English-dominated society, but luckily, my family had the resources to do everything possible for me to maintain a bilingual identity.

In my sophomore year, my mother was offered a job at La Universidad Autónoma de Querétaro in central Mexico. My experience at a private Mexican high school was very different from my year at a large urban public high school. At Berkeley High, I was considered too light-skinned, too green-eyed, too studious even, to possibly be Mexican-American. I remember being asked to read aloud in Spanish class, and looking up to my classmates staring at me, thinking, "Where did that white girl learn that Spanish!" In Mexico, I was accepted for who I was: a light-skinned, green-eyed, bilingual Mexican American with college-educated parents. No one did a double-take when I spoke Spanish. In fact, it was the opposite; everyone wanted to know where I had learned English so well. I have had the opportunity that most Mexican-Americans will never have: exposure to a high academic level of Spanish. I read books, wrote papers, even won a public-speaking award in a language I had once only associated with talking. As a result, I am able to articulate myself both orally and academically to a very wide variety of people.

This certainly came in handy the summer En Pointe traveled from Berkeley to Mexico to participate in a dance and cultural exchange. I was in charge of making arrangements with hotels, language schools, and rehearsal space for the twelve dancers and six parents, as well as putting together publicity, and emceeing two performances. Being onstage, speaking out to a full house filled with both Mexicans and Americans, I felt a level of comfort that reaffirmed my identity not only as a truly bilingual person, but also as a bicultural one. Backstage with the dancers, my American sense of time kicked in as I nervously rushed them through makeup and costume changes between dances. However, as soon as I stepped past the wings, it was as if my Mexican self took over; I spoke calmly and warmly, never once worrying about how many seconds there were left, but simply enjoying the present moment.

BEN CHAMBERS (class of 2002) graduated from Claremont McKenna College in 2006 and is working as a manager of business operations at Facebook in Menlo Park, California.

My first day on the job, I walked in on pure chaos. The phones at the mayor's office rang incessantly, while reporters paced the hall, peering through the cracks in the blinds hoping to hear a comment from Berkeley's mayor, Shirley Dean. Word had gotten out the day before that the city's most powerful landlord was smuggling girls into the United States from India for prostitution and that two of them had recently died. The chief of staff briefed me on the situation, and then directed me to hunt through local newspapers for information relevant to the case. Sitting there with my highlighter in one hand and a pair of scissors in the other, it occurred to me I had been thrown into the thick of a political scandal and was loving every minute of it.

Since this stark first taste of politics, I have interned at Mayor Dean's office for three years, and helped the office struggle through two more media outbreaks. Following September 11, 2001, Berkeley has been under intense public scrutiny; first, the Fire Chief ordered oversized American flags to be taken off fire trucks, and later, the City Council passed a resolution denouncing the U.S. military efforts in Afghanistan. Most of the public response and media attention was directed at the mayor's office. My assignment has been to assess thousands of e-mails and hundreds of phone calls from citizens across the country and the world, either berating the city and its "yellow-bellied, pot-smoking, communist leaders" or commending them for their bold statement. My findings help the mayor anticipate the repercussions to the city. Spending an afternoon each week in such a power hub has been a stimulating experience for me, giving me firsthand knowledge of the difficulties of running a municipal government and the passionate battles between moderate and radical factions that make governing more difficult. I now avidly read *The Berkeley Daily Planet* to follow local political developments.

Working at the mayor's office has intensified my interest in political science, leading me to take as electives Politics and Power, AP Economics, and AP Government at Berkeley High, as well as a Political Science course at Vista Community College last summer. Fascinated by the government policies and infrastructure that drive societies and economies, I am now strongly considering future studies, internships, and a career in government or economics.

Observing my budding political interest, the mayor's chief of staff suggested I serve on the City of Berkeley Youth Commission. The mayor appointed me to it, and in the two years since then, I've learned what it's like to actually be a public official instead of just supporting one. As a commissioner, I've worked on various youth-related projects such as installing a drug and alcohol mentoring program in middle schools and setting up a radio station at Berkeley High. I currently lead a subcommittee organizing workshops and forums that educate students about California's recently revised juvenile justice system and what their rights are as minors.

Besides giving me a chance to soak up experiences, my time spent in City Hall has allowed me to realize skills and talents I already have to offer. The mayor's office is run by five middle-aged, computer-illiterate women, and just about every week, I put my computer and Internet expertise to work for them. I have taught the staff how to enhance documents using outside images, restructured their system's hard drive to speed up access to files, and reformatted important letters and graphics to meet the mayor's exacting standards of visual presentation.

Interning at the mayor's office has provided me an opportunity to serve my community, broaden my horizons for the future, participate in actual politics, and build self-confidence. On top of all this, I have a fun time there, and throughout the week, look forward to whatever adventure I will take on next. Besides, not many high school students get to discuss with their mayor who the next outcast from *Survivor* will be.

Casey Laird (class of 2007) graduated from UC Santa Cruz in 2011 in American Studies.

The first section I turn to in the *San Francisco Chronicle* is Nation and World, usually dominated by Iraq, Afghanistan and Iran. But occasionally I see an article about Africa, South America or Asia, telling of a disaster destroying the homes of thousands of impoverished people, or the latest numbers on disease and illness spreading across the Third World. When I read these articles, images of smiling faces of friends in Shirati, Tanzania, or tentative, nervous smiles from street children selling gum in Morelia, Mexico, come to mind. I read the stories and think about people I've met living in these situations, how their destitute surroundings have dictated their lives, and how the adversities facing them only continue to rise. At the same time, though, these articles leave me frustrated, as they only tell one side of the story.

In the summers before my junior and senior years, I had the chance to go on extended trips abroad—to Morelia, Mexico, for a month and Shirati, Tanzania, for five weeks—through the small school-within-a-school, Communication Arts and Sciences, I attend at Berkeley High. Going to Morelia was the first trip I'd been on without my family, and it was quite a leap of faith for me. The other ten kids and I lived with Mexican families. We spent our days learning Spanish at an international language school and our evenings helping Mexican college students make videos about social issues facing the city, country, and world.

The following summer, twelve other students, two teachers, and I raised more than $30,000 to go to Shirati, Tanzania, a village of about 4,000 on the edge of Lake Victoria, where we taught HIV awareness and helped out at the regional hospital.

Both trips opened my eyes to another world. All my life, I've known that abject poverty existed, but it never seemed real to me. Poverty was a vague concept that was sad, and of course somebody should do something about it, but it never felt real. The people living in the "Third World" were always just numbers that I couldn't attach any real feeling to.

Meeting 8-year-old kids with grimy faces and hands, who spend their entire days selling gum to drivers of passing cars, while I helped make a movie about street kids in Morelia, made this poverty real to me. Working in an African hospital where frequent power failures can mean that emergency surgery must be completed by flashlight, or if there are no batteries, the pale glow of a cell phone, brought the reality of the human beings experiencing this life every day home to me. Now, reading articles about the spread of cholera or the rise of homelessness brings real faces to mind.

That's only half the story, however. Newspaper articles make problems like AIDS, hunger, and contaminated water seem insurmountable, impossible to rectify. That's not the case though, I now know. Small-scale, incremental efforts do make a difference, and small, dedicated groups can help to better lives in the Third World. One group of students or teachers may not be able to stop the spread of disease in Africa, but we did replace the damaged and missing mosquito screens in the hospital, so that newborn babies won't be attacked by mosquitoes and infected with malaria. We can come home with a plan to raise more money to provide a generator for the hospital, so patients can have reliable electricity. As an individual I can make small, positive changes that will make a big difference in the lives of other people.

CLAIR LEVY (class of 2002) graduated from
Emory University and received her PhD in microbiology
from Edinburgh University. She is working on a postdoc
at Scripps College, on a National Institutes of
Health fellowship on cancer research.

Thwack, went the sound of a wooden dildo hitting the side of a desk in
order to get the attention of my students. The room filled with shocked
gasps, and everyone's eyes cringed.

When I first considered becoming a Berkeley High peer health educator, dread and interest coursed through me. When I was a freshman,
I was downright shy. Even around my closest friends, I couldn't bring
myself to make a decision for fear that I might be criticized. The Peer
Health class at Berkeley High was created in order to teach students
public-speaking skills, as well as have the students talk to their peers
about subjects about which they wouldn't be comfortable talking to an
adult. I signed up, the only freshman in the class, ready to be trained to
teach senior guys the proper way of putting on a condom.

On the first day of class, I realized not only was I the only freshman,
I would be expected to talk to students about subjects that they might
not feel comfortable discussing with an adult. At this point, I didn't feel
comfortable discussing some of these topics either. Excitement, dread,
and curiosity filled my head. My first few presentations were very difficult, but eventually I was able to make presentations in Social Living
classes at Berkeley High, in the city's three public middle schools, and
at various private schools. My heart felt like it was going to jump out of
my chest every time I had to facilitate a group of seniors discussing the
many types of birth control, including demonstrating the proper way of
putting on a condom. I grew more in that semester than at any other time
in my life. The way I saw myself, as well as the way I perceived others to

see me, changed a lot. Now that I'm a senior, I find it amusing to imagine a freshman talking to me about birth control. I also find it amazing that I was able to talk about such mature matters. Talking about sex in front of up to ninety people (some of whom would rather be anywhere but there) just doesn't sound like something I would ever do, which is why it's so surprising to me that I'm still doing it in my senior year.

The class that taught me to be a Peer Health Educator had grant funding that ended after my freshman year. Since then, the program has been an extracurricular activity. As a sophomore, my group's focus was pregnancy prevention. I was again the youngest in the group, but I had come to like that role. I had friends who were juniors and seniors, and when you're a sophomore, it's nice to have friends in high places.

At my school, sophomores are required to take the Social Living class. So I had to make presentations in front of most of my friends and classmates from preschool on. Can you say embarrassing? One of my friends actually made up a song about me after I made a presentation in his class, and would sing it to me when we passed in the halls. Sophomore year was really hard for me. I'm not sure why or how, but I was pretty depressed for about six months that year. I felt that my life was slipping out of my control, but when I was presenting in all those classrooms, the control came back and I had some purpose. The only thing I remember looking forward to that year was presenting in the Social Living classes, where I had some control over what was going to happen.

By the end of my sophomore year, I was feeling normal again. Unfortunately, most of the other educators in the program graduated, which left only three experienced presenters with a new advisor. The three of us had to teach our new advisor how to run the program, as well as recruit and train new presenters. I took a leadership role in recruiting people for the program and then teaching them the curriculum. That year, I learned how to be a supervisor and how to solve problems with inexperienced educators.

So I ask again to the class, in what condition does the penis have to be in before putting on a condom? Everyone now yells out, "Hard!" Volunteers come up to stand beside me in the class with a wrapped condom in hand. I ask them to tell the class each specific step of putting on a condom. Repeating the step before they actually do it, so that if they make a mistake, a student who catches it can make the buzzer noise and tell them what step they forgot. The volunteer can sit down when the condom is on the dildo without any air bubbles between the condom and "pine" and a pinched tip for the semen to go. Before the activity is done, the class must tell me why you would use a condom. The answer simply is: to save your life. And not just preventing you from getting a deadly disease like HIV, but to prevent pregnancy or a less serious STD that would change your life considerably. Our last activity of the class is to answer any questions that they've written down on index cards. These questions are so powerful because the students can ask whatever they want without being pinpointed. I help save lives.

COLIN EPSTEIN (class of 2004) graduated from Colorado College in 2008 and returned to Oakland, where he teaches circus, parkour and gymnastics. He dances with a number of dance groups in the Bay Area, manages Palanza Dance, and has produced his own show, *Constants and Variables*.

I walked away from the desk, holding my schedule for the upcoming year. Wait a minute, I thought. OK, American Lit., Econ. and Government. OK, Latin, AP Bio. and Photo. But *Dance*? There it was on my schedule: Beginning Dance. A class I hadn't requested, didn't want, and had no intention of taking. I resolved to see my counselor and change it as soon as possible.

I filled out a schedule change request form, and waited. And waited. And waited. During all this waiting, I stayed in the dance class.

I realized after the first month that the administration wasn't planning to let me switch. I also realized that I didn't really want to any more. The dance class opened a whole new world for me, a world of movement, rhythm, and expression. It opened a world of wonderful things that I want to be a part of for as long as I can.

I had no idea of what to expect going into that class. I had attended the dance shows at Berkeley High School during my freshman and sophomore years, but I had never imagined myself as a dancer. So I was unprepared for what happened in the dance class. To start, there were three guys. And about thirty girls. That was a completely new experience for me, being so much in the minority of a class. Every other class I had been in throughout my school years had been more or less evenly balanced between girls and boys. Then there was the work we did in class, which I had never heard of or imagined. At the beginning, we did a lot of contact improvisation, a very open form of dance that involves weight shifts, balance, and a shifting point of contact between two people. We did things like leaning into or away from our partner, far enough that we were entirely off our center of gravity, finding places to balance on our stomach on a partner, and exploring ways of getting over, around, and through the partner while keeping the point of contact. I think this was a perfect introduction to dance for me, because it was very open, and more athletic, and close to what I had done in the past.

Eight months after that blessed computer error, I found myself backstage, waiting to dance in front of a packed house of about 300 people in Berkeley High's Little Theater. I had dropped a history elective in order to take Dance Projects, a student-run class that ends with an entirely student-choreographed show near the end of the semester. I was waiting, very nervously, to go onstage for my first dance. I guess I was talking out loud to myself, trying to calm down, and my friend Simon turned to me and whispered, "Dude, chill out. It's just like in rehearsal. Only this time, there's a whole bunch of people watching you."

"Gee, thanks, Simon, that makes me feel so much less nervous."

"Colin, you really need to calm down. Relax. Enjoy yourself. That's why you dance, isn't it?" another friend piped up.

And I had to admit they were right. The main reason I was standing onstage was because I wanted to have fun. Throughout my life, I've played baseball, a little soccer, a little football, done gymnastics, rock climbing, and various other things too, but none of it was anywhere near as compelling to me as dance. Dance is that fun, and it's something that I discovered randomly and loved the experience enough to keep doing it, and enough to use my valuable summer time to take more classes and dance more.

To finish the story: Our show was amazing. I realized Simon was right, and being backstage was more nerve-wracking than being onstage. You can't really see the audience, and the rehearsals took over, even through the nervousness that accompanied me onto the stage for my first dance, and before I realized it, I was head-over-heels into a cartwheel at the right moment, and thinking about something entirely different. We danced our hearts out, and the full house loved it, both on Friday and Saturday nights. When the waves of applause washed over the stage, the sheer exhilaration and adrenaline rush I felt was something I had never before experienced. As we wrapped up the show on Saturday, I thought about how far I had come: from someone who was put in a dance class by mistake and wanted desperately to transfer out, to a different person who willingly put on a show for friends, family and others and danced for fun. It's funny how life works out that way sometimes.

CRISTINE TENNANT (class of 2006) spent part of her junior year at the Mountain School of Milton Academy, in Vermont. She graduated from Whitman College in 2010, spent some time as a work-and-learn education resident at Shelburne Farms, Vermont, and now works for the Edible Schoolyard in Berkeley.

It was still dark out, and the freezing temperature chilled my California bones. I walked up the winding snow-covered path, the hill just steep enough to get my blood pumping. The sun was starting to rise over the Green Mountains of Vermont, and a sharp breeze pierced my lungs. In my left hand, I carried a yellow basket, and I used my right to pull open the heavy wood door of the chicken coop. When I stepped inside, I was met with both the warmth of the heat lamps and the acrid smell of soiled sawdust and chicken feed. As I approached the hens' nests, a few of the birds looked up at me. One or two ruffled their feathers. Mostly, though, they just ignored me. A particularly scrawny hen followed at my feet, ever hopeful for some extra grain. The air was thick with dusty feathers and gentle clucking. I began to collect the eggs, one by one, counting them aloud as I carefully put them in my basket. Every egg was different—some smaller, some larger. Most were brown, but occasionally one had a violet or green hue. Some of the eggs had just been laid, and I felt their warmth through my thick work gloves. "Sixty-three! Good work, ladies!" I said, to no one in particular. As I carried the now full basket towards the door, careful not to step on anyone in my path, I prepared myself for the cold outside.

Later, when I was washing the eggs in the harvest kitchen, I thought back to the many times I had eaten, cooked, or even looked at an egg without knowing exactly where it came from. Just three months earlier, I had been working as a short-order cook at Ozzie's, an original 1950s soda fountain in Berkeley, where French toast and egg salad sandwiches were our specialties. Countless times, I cracked open a cold egg onto the sizzling griddle and asked the customer sitting at the counter, "How do you like 'em—over easy or sunny side up?" Never did I contemplate the eggs themselves; I was too busy making sure that no chocolate milkshakes were forgotten and every customer was a happy customer.

A city girl born and raised, I never expected I would learn to love being a farmer. But there I was, using my hard-earned summer bucks to help pay for a semester at a farm school, and feeling more at home in the country than I did in the city. I had been excited about all the challenges of boarding school—leaving my family, living with a roommate, the stimulating academics, a Vermont winter, hard farm labor, and new friendships, but I never imagined that collecting chicken eggs would show me such a deep appreciation for the food I eat.

Today, almost a year later, I realize what a profound influence my time on the farm has had on the direction of my life. I am eager to experience rural life, and learn how to preserve the environment through sustainable farming. I now have an idea of what I want to do with my life. Eggs were just the beginning.

DANIELLE GOODMAN-LEVY (class of 2005) graduated from Vassar College in 2009 and worked, among other things, for President Barack Obama's re-election campaign in Las Vegas. In fall 2013, she was due to start law school at American University in Washington, D.C., on a public interest/public service fellowship.

The bright lights of the crowded restaurants illuminate the way, as we coast down Shattuck Avenue. I listen and laugh as my friend Jessica presents her latest boyfriend dilemma. We both jump when my cell phone explodes into "Hava Nagila," the Jewish song that is my phone's ring. Grabbing it from my bag, I read "Home" flashing on the screen.

"What now?" I say jokingly, expecting my Dad on the line to tell us not to stay out too late, or my Mom to tell us to drive carefully because there are a lot of drunk drivers on holiday weekends.

"Dani?" I hear fear in the muffled voice of my younger brother. "Dani, you need to come home right now. Mom needs you."

Six years ago, before my brother's call, on a Friday afternoon in sixth grade, I knew I had had a wonderful childhood. That was also the day my Dad cried and cried. It was the day I hated my Mom for getting cancer. But after three surgeries and eighteen months of chemotherapy, the cancer was gone.

In October of my junior year, exactly five years after my mom's first cancer episode, it came spinning back, messing up everything with the whirlwind of terror, sadness, and lack of control that it brought into our lives. Writing poetry and crying became a daily routine for me.

Now, as I walk quickly through the gate and swing open the front door, I can sense my own fear. I am breathing too hard, and praying for something under my breath—or for not something. With my fingers crossed on one hand, I run upstairs to my parents' room. My mom lies paralyzed in pain on the bed, her usually rosy pink cheeks turned white. I should have expected it, it is the second day after the chemotherapy—day two is always the worst.

My Dad has gone out for medicine; my brother sits terrified. "Wes, go get her a glass of cold water." I know he needs an escape; 14 is too young to deal with this. I move toward my mom, my breaths as quick as if I had just run five miles.

I sit with her for a long time, occasionally rubbing her back or running my fingers through her practically nonexistent hair—"the worst part of chemo," she says. I know that there are worse things, though, when you've been through what she has, but the lack of hair is a reminder of the tragedy.

The hardest part for me has been my powerlessness—the fact that there is nothing I can say or do to keep my Mom alive. And although she is a fighter, how much can you fight cancer before it eventually takes control and runs its own course?

My nickname on my rugby team is "Captain Mom," partly because of my leadership as team Captain, and partly because I take care of people—by now, I am good at it. And in a big way, helping others lets me forget my own pain and allows me to feel good about making a difference in other people's lives. I have found this through coaching a little girls' soccer team for the past two years, and focusing my energy on my girls' needs.

I sit there taking in the soft baldness of her head, the place on her face where her eyebrows should be, the absence of her once beautifully long eyelashes, the ones I inherited. A steady flow of tears trickles down my hot cheeks, but I let them roll because there is nothing I can do to stop them. What I can do, though, is go on with my life and in my own way, try to make the world a better place: working hard at school and at my job, coaching, playing soccer and rugby, and pursuing social justice give me confidence and show me how strong I am.

DMITRI GASKIN (class of 2013) planned to attend Stanford University.

"In Max's room a forest grew and grew…" I played the piano alongside the orchestra as the narrator read from *Where The Wild Things Are*. I looked out at the hundred-plus people in the audience: This was my room, which had grown into a forest.

It had started in my living room in front of our black grand piano long before. As a young child, I fell in love with music. However, when it came to practicing the difficult passages, my own Wild Things appeared. My nightly piano practice often ended in tears. After years of struggle, I gradually learned to befriend my Wild Things. I also learned that while I enjoy performing, first and foremost I am a composer.

Initially, my compositions were short and simple. But by eighth grade, inspired by my favorite composer, Steve Reich, I composed a forty-five-minute narrated oratorio that retells the story of the *Odyssey*; the piece won a national ASCAP Young Composer Award. The next summer, I attended a music summer camp in upstate New York—near where Reich lives. Determined to meet my idol, I wrote him several times with samples of my work. Finally, he agreed.

"No matter how spectacular your music is," he told me at his house, "it's not worth writing if it's never heard." Reich emphasized the importance of having my music played. Those words were my inspiration, the seeds to my forest.

Soon after meeting Reich, I founded an organization called Harmonikos. The mission is simple: help young composers of contemporary music have their music played. I invited other young composers to join. I organized and hosted rehearsals and board meetings, created postcards and programs, and built a website. At times, being executive director has also meant pestering procrastinating composers, giving orders to professional musicians in rehearsals, and reining in chatty teenagers to perform in a flash mob; despite the challenges, I continually pushed the organization to reach higher.

The forest I planted flourished: our concerts and group of composers grew, and our audiences with them. Each concert funded the next, eight in total so far. For one, we memorialized the victims of the 9/11 World Trade Center attacks with an oratorio for a large ensemble; for another, we staged live music to a viewing of a thirty-minute documentary I had been commissioned to score; for yet another, we commemorated the passing of Maurice Sendak in a piece I co-wrote.

In all, I'm proud to have created such a successful organization, especially since the path was not always smooth. Through Harmonikos, I not only succeeded in getting my own music heard, but I created a vibrant musical community that has sparked passion in many others.

Dᴏᴍɪɴɪᴄ Cᴀᴛʜᴇʏ (class of 2004) was able to set the first swim record in Berkeley High's new pool weeks before he graduated. He graduated from UC Berkeley and is working with a Bay Area nonprofit designed to support youth in the juvenile system and help connect them to sustainable resources within the community.

The summer I turned 12, it was hot. My cousin Jamie and my brother Lance and I wanted to go to the local swimming pool. We packed up our stuff and started walking, quiet, but excited. My cousin remembers that my face lit up with joy every time I heard the words "pool" or "water" come from my little brother's mouth. Like lightning striking from the sky, the sweat falling from my face was worth every moment of going to the pool that day.

We waited in line for fifteen minutes before the lifeguard came out to give the line of children a long reading of the rules and regulations. My mind wandered. Gazing off, I thought how the water would feel against my body. My soul was lifted when I heard the lifeguard say, "OK, that's the end of the rules." The line moved forward and, with my blood sparkling like champagne, I completely forgot about my cousin and little brother. All I could think about was the water. I ran through the locker room towards the pool. I couldn't control all the energy stored inside my body. The lifeguard blew the whistle to start the fun. Everyone jumped into the pool with their teeth shining like pearls, they were so excited.

Leaping into the shallow end of the pool, my cousin and I fell into a group of children splashing around, and that's when I saw the deep end of the pool and I knew that was where all the fun was. All I could think about was touching the bottom of eleven feet. I asked one of the lifeguards how I could get over there. My stomach muscles tightened up as I waited for his response.

"You have to take the test; four widths across the pool without stopping and then tread water for one minute." His eyes were still watching the pool as he told me this.

"Can I try?" Intimidated by what was ahead, I started to feel the sweat run down my face, and the sun didn't make it any better.

"Yeah, go ahead." He nodded with an OK, and so did I. I was 12 years old. I had never had a swim lesson. I had never swum in a pool before. The journey began, and acceleration went through my body. It was like rubbing my feet across a carpet before having the electricity run through my body once I'd touched a doorknob. Or the first time ever being sexually intimate with someone. As I finished the test, I looked up at the lifeguard once more with the same smile on my face.

"How was that?" I asked with deep, fast breaths coming from my mouth.

"Yeah, hey, that was great. You ever thought about being on a swim team before?" Now you could finally see his eyes. They were sparkling like sparkling wine that had just been opened.

Since then, I've swum competitively for eight years on the Oakland Undercurrent Swim Team and for four years at Berkeley High. I've learned that life's successes often come in small increments. Sometimes even the act of showing up at a workout when your body and psyche are worn out separates a great result from a failure. Swimming has shored up my determination to succeed. But, even more important, when I'm swimming a lap up and down the pool in practice, I feel as though it's one of the most peaceful places I've ever been. I can hear the waves crashing against the edge of the pool. There's no one to ask me, "Why aren't you doing this?" Or "Why aren't you doing that?" All I can hear is the wind blowing through my hair, and I get the feeling of water flowing around my body.

DORRIE SWANSON (class of 2003) studied at Tulane University in New Orleans. A registered nurse, she completed the Master's Entry Program in Nursing (MEPN) at the University of California, San Francisco, and is now there completing a two-year Master of Science in Nursing and Family/Mental Health Nurse Practitioner program.

Every Friday, I find my thighs sticking to the school's plastic chairs. I spend half of class tugging at my pleated skirt so that it strategically covers as much skin as possible. Friday is Game Day, and, as a cheerleader, I show my school spirit by wearing my uniform. I have all the makings of an ideal cheerleader: blonde hair, a playful attitude and lots of rhythm. However, at Berkeley High, I am all wrong.

In between classes, my arms are loaded with books as I maneuver my way through the hordes of students to my next class. As a friendly person, I instinctively smile at students I know and even those I do not. I am hit with shouts of, "There goes the white one," as though it is a rare sighting of an endangered species. This is annoying, but I have realized that it is not personal; it is a reflection of the racial climate at Berkeley High. It is a segregated environment behind an integrated facade.

The bell for lunch rattles and the students flock into the courtyard. On "the steps" are the masses of white students meeting each other for lunch. On "the slopes" is the sea of black students doing just the same. Venture into any classroom, and it is clear that Berkeley High students separate themselves. There are traditionally segregated extracurricular activities as well. The white kids populate sports such as crew and lacrosse, whereas black students dominate sports like football and cheerleading. Despite all the efforts to bring students together, Berkeley High School remains, in actuality, racially divided. As a white cheerleader, I am crossing this not so invisible racial line.

I first saw the Berkeley High cheerleaders at Freshman Orientation and was completely in awe of their performance. It was like a finely staged music video, as opposed to the usual cheerleading series of stunts and jumps. On the day of cheerleading tryouts, I, a freshman eager to learn the dance routines, was one of sixty girls. I had been dancing since I was able to walk, and as I got older, I found my love for hip-hop. My dance classes were lacking stimulating material, and I thought that cheerleading would provide challenging and innovative choreography. I was anxious to expand my repertoire.

The morning of cheerleading tryouts I was glued to the mirror, the radio blaring, as I repeatedly practiced the routine, swinging my hips to the fast-paced beat. On the way to school, I found myself fantasizing a stunning performance, with comments like "She was phenomenal" and the reward of a bouquet of spring flowers as victorious music played in the background. What a shock! I was greeted with looks of confusion and anger—I did not belong there; cheerleading was not a "white" thing. By the time the coach posted the roster and I was one of two white girls who had made it onto the varsity squad, I felt as though all the girls hated me. I was invading a space that already seemed small and sacred to them. I felt both discouraged and alienated by the rejection, but I was also unwilling to give up. "Wrong" or not, I was determined to be a cheerleader.

In the course of three days practicing on the rust-colored track, with footballs whizzing over our heads, we learned an eight-minute dance. Next it was time for solo performances in front of all the cheerleaders and the gawking football team. Solo performances? More like a way to prove our worthiness to be squad members, I thought. Dance was the only way I could break the ice and give them a glimpse of who I was. My stomach was in my throat, and my teeth were chattering. I heard the "5, 6, 7, 8" and, having nothing to lose, I let myself go. The energy in the group shifted from hostility to excitement. Samantha yelled, "She's hittin' it!" Shanae screamed, "That girl has rhythm!" Soon, I was no longer performing alone but dancing with the squad as they pulsated and clapped to the beat, shouting in unison, "Go, white girl, go, white girl ..."

Over the last four years, we have helped each other learn routines and polish our style. A sense of camaraderie developed because we developed respect for each other and realized we were all there for a common goal: to cheer on the team. I did not go out for cheerleading to defy racial barriers or to learn something about the loneliness of being a minority. I did not stick with it in order to learn about perseverance. Granted, along the way I did learn about those things, but the best part for me is that I made new friends who are vivacious and caring. I am a cheerleader because I love to dance and be with my friends. While the racial climate at Berkeley High is tense, when it comes to cheerleading, being black or white no longer separates us. With only three games left in my last season, I am glad I did not let what has been commonly accepted to influence me in my decisions, my friends, and what I choose to do. My feistiness took me from being the "white girl who can dance" to Dorrie, the friend they call on the weekends to invite to family barbecues.

ELEANOR SMITH (class of 2000) graduated from Dartmouth College in 2004. She is a senior staff editor at *The Atlantic* magazine in Washington, D.C., and still starts her day reading several newspapers, albeit now online.

The *San Francisco Chronicle* and *The New York Times* mean as much to me in the morning as a cup of coffee does to others. It is not my alarm but the pull of the morning newspaper that gets me going. At the breakfast table, I drink my juice, fill a bowl with cereal, and arrange the paper so that it is perfectly propped up against two blue candlesticks. Only then do I give myself the pleasure of opening the paper. I have to admit that I start with the entertainment section: the Datebook. I read the comics, several columns, and tidbits such as "Who Said What." I usually have a couple of chuckles as I check out whom Doonesbury is making fun of today and what snippy advice Miss Manners is dishing out. After the humor section, I move to the news. I never get over how much can happen in one day alone. The news can be moving, shocking, frustrating, even thrilling.

What excites me most about the newspaper is how it connects the whole. Every day I read articles not only about my own city and country, but also about the entire world. I love how the newspaper presents new ideas to me and leaves me thinking. When I read the newspaper, I don't forget the articles I read. I think about the issues and read the follow-up articles. I discuss them with my family and friends. I am especially attracted to issues that I've learned about either from my personal reading or from my schoolwork. For example, I recently read the book *Dead Man Walking* by Sister Helen Prejean. It awakened me to the problems in the United States' judicial system and to the death penalty. I read articles related to these issues with growing interest. Recently, I have started to collect newspaper clippings and magazine articles on various topics in which I am interested. I have a stack of articles on everything from the history of

World War II to current topics such as gun control.

My love of reading the newspaper did not come out of the blue; when I was little, my parents read to me. I was not such an attentive listener as I am now. While my mom would try to read to my two older sisters, I would jump from my parents' bed into the air, forcing my oldest sister to leap up and catch me over and over again. But as the years went by, books began to lure me. I still remember begging my mom for "Just one more chapter" at bedtime and when I was older, pausing during homework, to hear the story being read aloud to my younger brother.

Joining my school newspaper was a natural for me. The Berkeley High *Jacket* is not a standard school paper. *The Jacket* is an award-winning paper with some fifty students on staff. It comes out every other week and runs from 16 to 20 pages, with a circulation of 3,500. During my sophomore year, I worked on the business staff. That spring I applied to be managing editor, the position that I still hold. As managing editor, I have a vote on the editorial board and am in charge of production, management, and the paper's finances, including raising and managing a budget of $20,000, all of which comes from ads and subscriptions. I learned how to deal with difficult people at the printing press, complaining subscribers, and the school accountant. I transferred bookkeeping to a computer and spent more time at school than most kids would be able to imagine. Being managing editor is in a sense the best of two worlds. I am involved in the writing side of the paper as well as the production and management side. I like being in the middle of the action. I am the one people come to when they want to buy a computer hub. I am also the one who says "no" to the insistent staff requests for a refrigerator, microwave, sofa, and even a karaoke machine. However, sometimes I think that maybe my other title should be "Manual Editor." After all, I am the person, who carries all the newspapers in from the delivery car, my hands smudged with newsprint. But I'm not complaining. I like newsprint: its cheap smell, gritty feel and the pleasure it brings me.

ELI MARIENTHAL (class of 2004) graduated from Brown University in 2008 and is working on a PhD in human geography at UC Berkeley, studying the politics of humanitarianism and the political economy of disaster in Haiti. He continues to write and work as an actor performing original work.

Jesse, Dave and I had camped on the western slope of the ridge the previous night. Shaded by the mountain from first light, we awoke later than normal, not rising until the sun was high enough to reflect brightly off the lake below. Skipping breakfast, we quickly filled our water bottles and headed out towards the southern ridge of Graveyard Peak in the central Sierras. My two closest friends, both of whom were leaving for college the following week, and I have made several important journeys together. This backpacking trip was to be our last for a long time, and the sense of love, companionship, adventure, and imminent loss it entailed had whipped us into a state of continual exuberance. We were just so glad to be with one another that everything was perfect, every occurrence a small miracle. We were in love with life, with the mountains, and with our friendships.

That morning Jesse put into the daypack: water, granola bars, his sweatshirt, and a mango. This was an unusual item to have, because as any avid backpacker knows, a mango makes a bad traveling companion. It's heavy, perishable, and messy. We had brought it almost as a joke, dubbing it the celebratory mango. Unsure just what we were going to celebrate, we knew nonetheless that it was an essential ingredient in our journey. For twenty miles, we had coddled it, protected it, packed it delicately and carefully, and now it was coming to the summit, up 2,000 feet where the snow never melts and only the bravest birds dare perch. After three hours of scrambling over boulders and crawling through vast patches of gooseberry and young manzanita, stopping occasionally to rest against the trunk of a secure foxtail pine, we reached the summit.

The treeline broke to expose the untamable grandeur and immense beauty of the High Sierras. Jesse brought out the mango and handed it to Dave, who gently drew back the skin to reveal an unbroken sphere of golden flesh. When it was split into thirds, the fruit-covered pit saved to be shared later, we delved into our mango. We quickly ate the bulk of our portions, slowing down only to lick the juice from the palms of our hands, using our teeth to pull the small strings of fruit that had been pushed under our nails as we devoured our celebratory mango. As we sat there, sticky and content, I asked rhetorically how anything could be so good. Jesse looked at us contemplatively and said, "I've never allowed a mango to get that ripe before. Usually I eat it as I leave the store. But we've waited four days for this moment, savored the idea of that mango for so long, given it time to ripen, and now we've eaten the best thing that has ever been."

I have devoured these past seventeen years, loved them and cherished them. They have left me ecstatic about the possibility of many more. Yet I think I'm going to slow down now, lick life's nectar gently from the palm of my hand, acknowledge the importance of sitting still, cherish the lyricism within the epic of my life and the detail within the bigger picture. I am simply going to allow things to ripen. That which is most precious—love, art, fruit—needs only to be stewarded, given a chance to ripen in the dark unknown of the heart, or of the mind, or even the depths of an old metal-frame backpack.

ELLEN CUSHING (class of 2006) graduated from New York University in 2010 and works as a staff writer and web editor for the *East Bay Express*. This essay discusses the death of Meleia Willis-Starbuck, a Berkeley High graduate. Meleia's college essay is included in this collection.

My world changed on July 17, 2005, and I changed with it.

As a child of Berkeley, California, the birthplace of the Free Speech Movement and the home of countless demonstrations about everything from veganism to the war in Iraq, I've always considered myself a politically conscious person. I attended my first protest rally when I was still in diapers, and I am passionate about a variety of political and social issues.

To this end, at the beginning of my sophomore year, I chose to enroll in Communication Arts and Sciences (CAS), a program within Berkeley High School that emphasizes social justice. I also joined the staff of our newspaper, *The Jacket*, and these two activities have been the biggest, best, and most important things I've done in high school. In CAS, I have been able to take classes that resonate with me and engage in valuable discussions, surrounded by perceptive and creative people. On *Jacket*, I have honed my skills and cemented my desire to write for the rest of my life.

These feelings and passions all converged when Meleia Willis-Starbuck, a Berkeley High alumna home on break from college, was shot and killed during the summer before my senior year. Grief and pain spread outward through the concentric circles of my communities: first CAS, which she was also a part of; then Berkeley High School; and then the entire Berkeley community. None of these communities is large, but they feel even smaller when something like this happens.

When the editorial board of The *Jacket* gathered to plan the first issue of the year, the mood was somber. We knew that the story of Meleia's death and life would be the focus of an issue usually dedicated to anticipatory stories about this year's football team, and I was both honored and intimidated when my fellow editors unanimously chose me to write the article—pleased that I had earned their respect, but worried that encapsulating Meleia's nineteen-year existence in a thousand words would be like stuffing an elephant into an earring box.

I learned from Meleia's friends and teachers what a leader she was both in and out of the classroom, and I heard stories about her leadership of Berkeley High School's Black Student Union, and her participation in domestic violence prevention efforts. I saw my history teacher, a man I admire immensely, choke back tears as he recalled Meleia's contributions to his class and the CAS community. And suddenly, I found myself mourning someone I had never met, someone I would never meet. It is heartbreaking to get to know and love and be inspired by someone after she is gone.

Meleia's commitment to social justice is what struck me the most. Her example moved me to become more involved with my community, to pay tribute to her not by simply writing an article, but by living a life she would have been proud of. I became a part of the newly formed CAS Race and Equity Committee and worked with a small group to plan a six-hour community-building workshop for the senior class. Once school started, I joined the CAS leadership class, and was then selected by my peers to be one of four students on the twelve-person CAS Leadership Council. In this group, I can help set the direction for my community by making decisions regarding budget, teacher hiring, and curriculum.

Learning about Meleia inspired me to be a better, more engaged, more active person, to turn this tragedy into something positive. Her days were cut short, so I want to make sure that I use each and every one of mine to effect change.

ELLIE LAMMER (class of 2004) graduated from
Tufts University in 2008, lives in Brooklyn, and is senior
producer and program manager for a London-based
innovation consultancy in Manhattan.

The dough is an extension of my hands as I push and spread its pliable mass over the worn countertop. Hip-hop beats pulse, lyrics intertwining with the sweet smells that waft through the house. In the oven, a chocolate soufflé bakes to perfection, the thin crust covering its rich, moist center. The aromas entice my friends to linger, and they bide their time playing cards. The kitchen is a tangle of people. My brother and his friends sneak tastes of the dough, as my parents welcome guests. The crowd impatiently awaits the beep of the timer. My ingredients are sloppily laid out on the counter, nonchalantly scooped into bowls by feel. "One cup of flour," reads the recipe, so I throw a handful into a bowl, followed by a pinch of baking powder. The ingredients mix and mingle with my schoolbooks, calculus equations sauté with conversations. My feet are bare and coated in flour, like my trusty red apron.

Years ago, I wore the same over-sized apron wrapped awkwardly around my small waist as I stirred a pot while teetering on the edge of a chair. I was fascinated with the mysteries of food, how batter becomes cake in the oven and how to cut an egg in half. My mom shared my passion, and remained calm as I wielded large knives and hovered over boiling pots. Her encouragement and trust inspired me to comb through cookbooks, experiment, and invent my own concoctions. My trademark dish is cake, which I studied in a course where I perfected the art of icing flowers, and in an AP Chemistry project on leavening agents. Sadly, I can't bake a cake every day, so when I come home at six after cross-country practice, a full day of school, and student government meetings, I help my mom cook dinner. The comforting smells of cooking food and the melodic rhythm of chopping vegetables slow the rush of my busy schedule.

Berkeley is a chef's paradise, with fruits, vegetables, and spices from around the world at my fingertips. In January 2001, when I packed my oversized bags for my family's sabbatical in Scotland, I had no idea what culinary challenges lay ahead. We lived in an ancient stone house in a village on the North Sea. The gloomy kitchen contained no more than a tiny box oven and a miniature refrigerator. I joined the crew team at my school and invited the girls over to teach them how to make chocolate chip cookies. The heat of the oven warmed up the dismal kitchen, and the cookies bridged the cultural gap between my new friends and me. Every year, when I go back to visit, I come armed with a supply of chocolate chips.

The mob in my kitchen becomes increasingly impatient, until finally the timer beeps, and I open the oven to reveal a chocolate masterpiece, warm and puffy. My brother pours milk for the throng, some of whom have sat around the table for so many years that they are no longer considered company. I sit down with the steaming soufflé and watch as lifelong relationships blend with budding friendships, and I bask in the beauty of food.

EMMA DONNELLY (class of 2002) graduated from UC Santa Cruz in 2010, worked as a Peace Corps volunteer in Cape Verde in West Africa, and is pursuing a master's degree at the University of San Francisco in teaching English to speakers of other languages.

The sun seeped into my hospital bedroom, its warmth spreading across my swollen eyes. Forcing myself to get up, I slowly moved my legs onto the floor. I gripped the cold steel bed-frame and stood up. Dizzy, nauseated, and alone, I walked towards the mirror, dragging a beeping machine behind me. I expected to see my familiar 10-year-old face with wavy brown hair and sunflower eyes, but the reflection I saw in the mirror was that of a stranger. I saw a girl with no hair and bruised skin, her only familiar feature her eyes. I took a deep breath. I was alone with a pitiful survivor. For one long moment, I felt immensely sorry for her, for myself. Looking at my reflection, I made a promise never to feel this way again. I did not want to spend the rest of my life in sorrow.

I began having flashbacks of the surgery. I remembered nurses rolling me down white hallways, pushing me into a room filled with bright lights and loud sounds. Strangers in blue masks and plastic gloves held my hands as they sedated me with a gas that smelled like burnt tires and root beer.

When I awoke, my Pop was holding my hand. "Do I look different, Pop?" I asked him. "Yes, but you are still Emma." I was told that I had survived a twelve-hour craniotomy, and was diagnosed with a rare bone disease called fibrous dysplasia. For the last six years, unknowingly, a tumor had been strangling my optic nerves, causing blindness in my left eye. Although the surgery was a success, and I could already tell an improvement in my vision, I had no way of knowing that two years later, my world would grow dim again. Every day it felt as if the sunlight was being turned down by an invisible dimmer switch. Dark shadows became my best friends, and I knew that my worst nightmare was coming true. I needed to have another craniotomy.

"Different" is who I have learned to live with. But in the process, I felt that I had to conceal this difference from most people because I wanted neither pity nor special treatment. My greatest desire, especially in junior high school, was to be "normal." Hiding my disability was essential because it was my chance to be in a new life. But there wasn't a day that I didn't think about my eyes. I have lived with this disability for nine years and convinced myself that how I see is normal. I have forgotten what it is like to see through both eyes, since I lost my vision in my left eye when I was 10. Nonetheless, with my remaining vision, my world is beautiful.

For a long time I searched desperately to find my passion, my special gift. I will never forget the day I walked barefoot across a smooth wooden dance floor. A woman with chocolate skin and renaissance hair walked into the room. Her presence saturated me with excitement and enthusiasm. Ms. James could leap like fire and twist like the wind. Inspired by this goddess, my dance teacher, it was my dream to be free like her. As days and months passed by, I began to love the sawdust scent of the dance room and crave the coolness of the wooden floor beneath the soles of my feet. Ms. James taught me how to express my whole being through motion instead of words. With this gift, she gave me the world.

Before I started dancing I had no place to release my anger, sadness, or joy. Dance freed me of my insecurities and became the voice with which I could express fear and courage, beauty, and grace. Two years later, when I auditioned for Dance Production at Berkeley High School, an intensely competitive and prestigious program, I was accepted. I could only marvel at my transformation from an insecure person to a leading dancer. In a short time, I had become a choreographer, lighting director, and costume designer. I had learned how to create unique and beautiful dances of my own.

Dancing fills me up with a wild rush of exhilaration. I am in a place where I am accepted, and no one could guess that this girl flying through the air has a disability. It is my secret, but I can't hide this secret from myself. I am constantly reminded each day of the path that I have traveled, and I am grateful. I do not know if or when I will need to have another craniotomy, but with this unknowing, I choose to cherish what I have now, the people in my life and my future. For myself, I have dance, because when I dance, I am in love.

EMMA SMITH (class of 2005) graduated
from Yale University in 2010, and is completing a
master's in public health and epidemiology at
UC Berkeley before returning to complete her medical
degree at the University of Southern California.

I am now a trapeze artist with the potential to realize a professional performing career, one of the few lucky ones who has actually had the opportunity to "run away and join the circus." When people ask me what I do after school and I reply, "I'm in the circus," they usually raise their eyebrows skeptically and conclude that I'm referring to a Ringling Bros., Barnum and Bailey-style show, complete with three sawdust-filled rings, parading elephants, and bags of roasted peanuts. However, most circus people now are part of the new wave, Cirque Nouveau, a theatrical spectacle that combines acrobatics, mime, juggling, contortion, trapeze, and other disciplines.

Since I was 7, my instructors, former Chinese acrobats, have told me "Training is bitter," but there are moments in performance that transcend it all. When I hang from the trapeze bar, adrenaline pulsing through my arteries, I forget the searing pain in my palms, the bruises I'm about to earn, the makeup sweating off my face, or how when I get off stage I have to find my juggling clubs for the next act. Right now, it's just the trapeze, the audience, and me. The theater is dark and all the lights are trained on me, glaring into my eyes, nearly blinding me. But I know the audience is out there watching. I can see the red eye of a video camera, the glint of someone's glasses. I feel their eyes fixed on me, and I smile back. I count the music and swing my body under the bar in as wide an arc as I can muscle. I pull up over the trapeze and, resting on my hips, slowly take both hands off, reaching out to that anonymous mass, who I know are waiting, torn between fearing for me at that great height and wanting to be scared. This is, after all, the chills and thrills of the circus. Finally, I fall forward into the trick until I am almost perpendicular to the ground. At the last possible moment, I whip in, riding the momentum of my fall, and spin all the way around the bar. I repeat the trick, gaining speed, listening to the little gasps of the audience. Every time I come around the bar, I look out, teasing them. I am in complete control at this moment. Finally, I throw both arms out to the crowd, hurling myself towards the ground, and at the very last instant, I snake one leg around the ropes, come to an abrupt halt, hanging by one hooked knee, head downwards, my hands blocking the fall I never make. The audience is terrified, but they love it. First afraid and now ecstatically satisfied, they break into applause, cheering for me.

People say "You can shake the sawdust out of your feet, but you can't shake it out of your heart." And it's true. Circus is deeply ingrained in my life and my heart. For me, there is magic in every performance.

ERIN ANDERSON (class of 2007) graduated from Yale University in 2011 and works as the director of marketing for a pharmaceutical company in New York.

It's been a long four hours, and I could use a break. The instant I sit down, though, my boss bursts through the swinging door. "We need more plates out there. And get that frittata on a platter. Has anyone started making coffee?" And with a clanging of dishes, she is gone.

Working in the kitchen of my synagogue is no small feat. Putting together an elaborate brunch for a hundred ravenous bar mitzvah guests requires focus and determination, not to mention endless patience. It takes aplomb to smear cream cheese on 200 bagel halves while nervous parents dart in and out of the kitchen, muttering "Do you think we'll have enough couscous?" and "Where's the coffee?"

When I started working in the kitchen, I was clueless. I leaned in a corner, waiting for my boss to assign me a chore. While scanning the kitchen, I glanced over at the sink. My gaze lingered on the frittata-flecked pans and cream cheese-smeared knives that spilled over onto the counter, and I knew what I had to do. I marched across the kitchen, rolled up my sleeves, and plunged my arms up to the elbows into the soapy water. My confidence rose with the pile of sparkling plates in the drain rack, and by the time I had emptied the sink, I was ready to take on the world.

Empowered by my success at dishwashing, I attempted more difficult tasks. Slicing pineapple, bussing tables, replacing empty cookie trays: I didn't want to stop for lunch. I worked through break, collecting plate after plate of brownie crumbs and picked-over salmon and loading them into the sink. While before I had shuffled awkwardly around the kitchen, I now strode efficiently, stopping only to pick up empty sugar packets and discarded teaspoons. And whenever I ran out of tables to clear, I marched to the sink, rolled up my sleeves, and started over.

It has been five months since I received my first paycheck, and I am not only comfortable in the kitchen but have learned to apply my catering skills to daily life. I attribute much of my newfound confidence and poise to the time I have spent by the sink. The unpredictable nature of kitchen work has taught me not a specific skill set, but rather a re-sourceful way of thinking in any situation. Social interactions, formerly my Achilles heel, are now no more intimidating than piles of dirty dish-es. Contributing voluntarily to class discussions is easier than clearing tables. I tackle a long and arduous economics test with the composure and persistence I employ when confronted with a mountain of bagels to slice. Prior to entering the kitchen, I thought that opportunities would simply fall into my lap, but now I know that I must seek them. I used to let the dishes pile up, but now I roll up my sleeves and get to work.

ERENDIRA GUTIERREZ (class of 2000) attended California State
University, Chico, and is a hair and makeup stylist, who
has worked for reality TV shows. She and her husband
have a wine bar on the Nayarit Riviera in Mexico.

When the door shut, it slammed so hard I heard the room echo. The
room looked so pale and cold, like something you would only see in the
movies. Everything was cement and tightly compacted. I sat on the thin
layer of cushion that was laid out on the bed for hours, asking myself a
hundred questions, repeating myself over and over.

My first idea was to escape. It hadn't kicked in that I had no options.
I tried to pick the automatic lock to my door. I even tried to think of a
way to melt the nine-inch-thick plastic window to get out. I wondered if
anyone even remembered that I was in this room or if I even existed.

The next morning I woke up to the horrible sound of the Juvenile
Hall guard's voice telling us to get up and make our beds. I had barely
opened my eyes, thinking my bad dream was over. But it wasn't—it had
just started.

I was so terrified about what was going to happen. I was in trouble
with the law and my family. I was more afraid of coming out than stay-
ing in. I was going to be dealing with the toughest family and teachers. I
had a lot to think about in forty-eight hours. I had a weird feeling about
worrying my teachers, as they had become a big part of my life. I never
thought I would even become close to one. I thought they gave me "F's"
because they just didn't like me. The truth was that I was at the best
high school, where teachers love their students and will take that extra
step to make sure that we succeed.

When I was 15, I could have sworn my birth certificate said 21. I
even got to live like an adult. But when I was 16, that's where it got bad
and my adulthood paid me back. "Erendira Gutierrez, please strip and
bend over. Then cough." Those were the words of the woman who left
me bare and cold and ashamed. Assault and robbery was what it was

called, for my case. The fingerprints, the mug shot, everything I've watched on *Cops* is what I experienced.

At the age of 15, I was known as a juvenile delinquent. Who would have ever thought I would follow in my brother's footsteps? Life was surrounded by gangs, in my eyes. I grew up in a neighborhood where the majority were Latinos who immigrated from all over Latin America. Gangs came in the late 1960s, which carried on from generation to generation. The people I looked up to and the people who I thought I could be with, the ones with the so-called power, were failures, gang members.

The four days I was in Juvie felt like four months. Every time they closed the doors behind me, I felt this bitterness that the system had the key to my life, and in reality it did. Who was I to blame at the age of 15? "The white man put me here," I thought, but the fact was I couldn't blame anyone but myself. It was the Chicana girl that put herself here.

The two people that I was mostly worried about were my aunt, Beatriz, and my teacher, Mr. Ayers. They both had done a lot for me to achieve. I was embarrassed and ashamed. They both had tried to keep me out of trouble, but there was nothing they could say or do to change my mind. I had to find it in my eyes. Two thoughts, giving in to my gang or proving myself for the rest of my life. It had to be one or the other that was more important to me.

When I was a little girl. I always wanted to be like my Tia Beatriz, who I thought was mean and smart, a very strong Chicana with a perfect family that included a dog. I could only think she was very lucky, but now I was starting to realize that it had nothing to do with luck. At this point, I had to think about what was best for me—having everything she had or not knowing if I was going to live the next day or not. I had to think if my gang was going to make me happy or if I should go to college, get a good job, education, and have a family of my own.

All these points laid out for me made me change so quickly. My outlook, my views, my friends, my attitude changed. Here I am today, May

1999, at UC Santa Cruz, getting some help from college students. They are helping me to write this college admission essay. Sitting with one of my classmates whom I hated during my sophomore year because I thought she was too smart, telling her my story and asking for her opinions.

I never once thought that I would make it this far or even visit a college to write an essay for my future. I'm thinking right now, and looking back, even if it was a few months ago, how stupid and selfish I was. I was making myself think I was going to become someone bigger with power. The real power is what good things you do with your life. I know that college is just the beginning of those good things for me.

EVAN NEFF (class of 2011) is a student at UC Santa Cruz.

"OK. It's painful today, but I can make it home." I hobble a block from school. The searing September sun beats down, and the mild pain becomes agony. I limp another block. Waves of pain radiate from my hips. I ease myself down on a stranger's stoop, take out my cell phone and call my mother.

Four months later, after seeing a half-dozen doctors in search of a diagnosis, my condition has a name: juvenile ankylosing spondylitis—advanced arthritis of the hips. I can no longer walk. While other sophomores negotiate school halls, I remain at home, sprawled in a beige La-Z-Boy recliner, engulfed by home school assignments, food crumbs, and mild desperation. I glance over at the multitude of Get Well Soon cards my friends have sent me. A particularly jovial card reads "Can't bear to see you sick." On the front of the card, a small cartoon teddy bear that has seen better days is slumped over a crutch, its brown furry leg in bandages. The bear stands solitary. A button eye hangs from its socket, dangling by a thread. Its fur is scuffed and dirty. Despite all of this, the teddy bear's stitched mouth is curved into a stubborn smile.

Its happy-go-lucky expression confounds me. How could this animal, abandoned by its owner and left to face the world alone, be so peppy? Were I a cartoon bear, I might be jolly too.

Months pass. My father serves me a kaleidoscopic cocktail of anti-inflammatory pills: deep marine blues, sea foam whites, twilight magentas, kelp greens, salmon pinks. In my sea of confusion, hope shines through. These pills will fix me.

It is June. From my chair, I peer through the window and see bright yellow oxalis flowers—a weed that has always qualified as a respectable flower in my mind. As children, my friends and I called the plant "sour grass" and loved to pick its flowers and suck on the stems. A single thought shoots through my mind. I must pick that flower. With recliner remote control in hand, I press the "up" button with firm determination. When the motorized chair has reached the end of its vertical extension, I ease myself up slowly, protecting my tender hip joints. Thanks to the medication, the stabbing pain is gone—but walking is impossible without support. The cold metal crutches are just out of arm's reach. They are usually handed to me by others and used only as a tool to get from recliner to wheelchair. Now, however, they are my mainstay. Outside, I hobble to the patch of earth from which the oxalis shoots. Although it is summer and the ground is parched and cracked, the flower stands strong. Its resilience amazes me. I want to be that flower. I want to walk. My stomach flutters in a jumble of excitement, fear, anticipation, and bliss—as if my emotions are competing for my acknowledgment. The crutches clatter on hot cement. My legs tremble. I jerk one foot forward, and the other follows. One foot forward, then the other. The oxalis flower—my souvenir of regained independence—will be placed in a glass on my bedside table.

Before my diagnosis, I believed that I would never walk again. Now, I treasure my restored freedom above all else. While some may take life for granted, I appreciate the little things, because I know what it is like to be deprived of them. During my confinement, I found courage and determination. I discovered the importance of family as a support structure and my empathy for others grew. By junior year, I had recovered from my illness and was ready to return to school. Being incapacitated for eight months made me enthusiastic about my new life. I took advantage of my recovered independence. In spring of my junior year, I began working with the Berkeley High School Theater Technician Crew. Soon after, I joined the Berkeley High School newspaper, *The Jacket*, as a multimedia editor. Through these opportunities, I have learned new technical skills, made new friends and collaborated with students from different branches of my school community. Looking ahead, I am excited about college. I plan to expand my learning, explore and perfect my filmmaking and photography skills and connect with the international art community. Eventually, I want to travel the world, documenting my experiences and illuminating global issues through digital media. Having survived the experience of being confined to a chair for eight months, I hope to impact the world through action.

GEOFFREY SHAMES (class of 2005) attended Boston University and lives in Hollywood, working at the Circle Talent Agency. He co-founded a promotion company in Boston and recently helped start a clothing company named Nghtbrnd. He writes about his dear friend Nic Rotolo, who died in the middle of their junior year.

It was going to be an adventure for the ages. As we were a group of four 17-year-old boys, our planning for the trip was almost nonexistent. On the last day of school, the boys and I were going to jump into our cars, go to the airport, and spend the whole summer in Europe. We were going to fly into England and stay there for a few days, then buy Eurail passes and explore all of Europe for the rest of the summer. That was the extent of our plans. The whole idea was for Nic, Slither, Sam, and me to explore the other side of the world—no plans, no parents, no end to the fun.

We were always planning things like trips to Europe. We had plans to start our own clothing company, plans on how we were going to be successful, even plans on where we were all going to be in fifty years. We always did everything together, and we were all as close as brothers and planned to stay that way for as long as possible. That was all taken from us one night with one, quick, static-filled cell phone call.

Around 9 p.m. on February 5, 2004, I picked up my phone to hear a single sentence that would change the rest of my life. As soon as I picked up the phone, there was a strange silence that made my heart skip a beat, and I knew this wasn't a social call. The next three words that came out of my friend's mouth are still echoing in my head as I write this. It's really amazing how three simple words can send your whole life into a downward spiral, even before you have a chance to really think about what is being said. When I picked up the phone all I heard was "Nic is dead."

Upon hearing those words, my heart instantly seized up and I lost control of the muscles in my legs, landing on the floor in complete shock and bewilderment. At first I denied the whole thing. The idea that a 17-year-old boy in the best shape of his life, using no drugs or alcohol, and with no history of heart problems, could collapse dead in an instant just made no sense to me. After a few minutes of disbelief, emotions coursed into my mind like a tidal wave. The best part of my life had just been stripped from me. By some twist of fate, my best friend had just died of a sudden massive heart attack while playing ice hockey, something he did all the time. My emotions went from anger and wanting somebody to blame, to absolute depression and not knowing what to do with myself. That night, all of us who had been close to Nic cried in one big mass of sorrow, and quite honestly, it brought us closer together than we ever had been before. Now we are more like a very close family than just a group of friends.

On the first Sunday of every month, we all meet at Nic's old house and have a dinner party in his memory. Every time, there will be a few people who are feeling depressed, and there are always people there to comfort them. I'm writing this essay right now having just returned from one of these Sunday night dinners at Nic's house. This dinner was especially significant because it happened to be on Nic's birthday, which would have been his 18th. We all went to his house and went through our normal routine of eating great food, telling jokes and old stories about Nic, and just generally being there for each other, but this time we also did something more. Since it was Nic's birthday, we all brought candles and went out to the backyard and sang "Happy Birthday" to him. It was the most amazing spectacle of people getting together and helping each other out that I have ever witnessed.

While losing Nic was the worst tragedy I have ever faced, I also learned a great deal about myself and people in general because of it. I have learned that it is important to live life to the fullest in every second you have, and to try to achieve as much as you possibly can in the time you have in your life. You never know when everything may be taken away from you, so you have to take action when the opportunity arises. I have learned that there is always somebody out there who genuinely cares about you and wants you to succeed in life, and that you can always count on them to be there for you through good times and bad. It is truly a beautiful thing.

GRACE GILL (class of 2005) graduated from the University of Southern California in 2009 and is working for the CMI/India/Climate Center in New York.

"Oiy! Come here, girl! You said you wanted curry, you're 17, now get yourself over here and help me make it! When I was your age," my mama shouted, "I made an entire buffet consisting of seven different main courses and one hundred rotis and gulaab jamans. You're going to college now, what are you going to eat there? I won't be there with you, you know! Come here now, Grace Gill!"

Considering that I don't have a middle or a long first or last name, the effect isn't that impressive. Perhaps ... "Come here, Jaswinder Patti Gill!" Note the difference.

OK, OK. Trudging my feet like a pack mule being sent to the slaughter, I enter the steamy kitchen. Immediately, my eyes start to water. The spices assault me. I am yanked by the arm, and a plate of onions, garlic, ginger, parsley, and green pepper is shoved under my nose. "Cut." *But Ma! ...* "CUT!" My beautiful, serene mother suddenly looks like a really angry Emeril Lagasse, the frenzied TV cook. Not that I mind cooking, I love to cook, but curry is like a woman, very fickle and high maintenance. Actually, it's like me. Curry is the culinary representation of *moi.*

I stare dumbfounded at the spices and slowly begin picking them up and awkwardly cutting them. Slice, slice, slice, sugar and spice make every dish nice. Oh hush up, Gill. Now is not the time to practice your rhyming skills. I had been practicing on my tabla, my beautiful Indian drum set, before I was kidnapped by my mother. Well, maybe I'll cook the curry to the rhythm of the tabla. Cut, cut, cut, slice and dice. DhaDha Dhina Tin, Na Tin Na Tin. Eyes screwed against the sting, I slice the ginger. The juice spurts out and smacks me in my eye. OWW! I hop to the rhythm of the drums in my Afro-Haitian dance class. Boom, boom-boom. In the living room, my father sits with his whiskey, watching TV. He laughs, and his great big belly shakes like a bowl full of jelly. He grins at me. He knows he can sit there in his glorious personage while the womenfolk cook. "Oh, you useless girl." My arm is pulled again, and I find myself face to face with the bubbling curry, with my eye twitching ferociously. I don't know what to say. It looks really yellow and hot and angry. Stir the curry. I take the ladle and stir, trying to soothe the savage beast.

My mom's Lata Mangeshkar is drowned out with Kanye West's new rap song, "Jesus," on the radio. "Jesus walks with me, with me." I hum to the lyrics. *No, not Jesus. You're not Christian. Guru Nanak walks with me, with me.*

I look at the curry. Now it's bearing a resemblance to the substance I eat. Feeling a little bouncy, I stir some more. Now I'm feeling rather … intrepid. The aroma of the spices mingle flavorfully in the curry, and the color takes on a golden hue. It thickens and bubbles softly. Absurdly pleased, I grin and catch the confused eye of my mother, who is staring at me. *I was thinking of this joke someone told me*, I stammer. Her raised eyebrows leave no doubt that she doesn't believe me. It's OK. Mama's always known I'm weird and a persistent daydreamer. The green leaves in the curry swirl about and add dimension and flair to the dish. My arms flex, and I move them rapidly, like the blades of the mixer, which are currently pulverizing more ginger.

At last, the curry has been tamed like poor Kate, though I don't think Shakespeare had curry on his mind when he wrote *The Taming of the Shrew*. Ah well, back to my drums. Now I can re-enter my haven. "Where you going?" My mother's softly inquired question makes the fine hairs on my neck stand on end. Sounds suddenly seem distant, like one of those dramatic scenes you see in the movies. "Girl, you haven't even started on the rotis yet!"

HANNAH SARVASY (class of 1999) graduated from Harvard University in 2003 and was a Fulbright Scholar in the Netherlands. She is a cartoonist and linguist, currently working on a grammar of the Nungon language of Papua New Guinea for her PhD dissertation at James Cook University in Australia.

"Graciousness," my mother spit, wild-eyed, "graciousness!" She whirled

and banged the pot onto a burner. I flinched at the clang of metal crashing against metal, but slunk back to my cello in the living room to investigate a particularly hard passage of the Haydn Concerto in D. It wasn't
my fault my name meant "graciousness." My mother had named me Hannah after her grandmother, and if that wasn't the best name for me, well,
whose fault was that? She certainly could not shame me into apologizing
for our argument by reminding me of the meaning of my name.

I was always glad that I had not inherited my surname as well from
my mother's side of the family. Her last name was Sondik, a name that
in old times was used to refer to the man who held the baby during
the Jewish circumcision rites: not exactly the most glamorous of titles.
From my mother's family, however, I did inherit rough-hewn stories of
the Jewish Old World.

My mother's aunt told us that a drunken muzhik (Russian peasant)
shot and killed her grandfather, leaving his eleven children orphans. Her
father, Zavel, was the youngest, at 2 years old. It so happened, my great-
aunt said, that Zavel and his brothers and sisters did pretty well as they
grew older (considering that they were orphaned, destitute, and Jews
living in Russia: thrice cursed!). One of Zavel's brothers suffered a severe
setback, however, while attempting to escape the compulsory Russian
military service. He went to a peasant charlatan for help, who gave him
a powder to rub in his eyes. She told him it would blind him temporarily for the duration of the Army examination, but the ensuing blindness
proved to be permanent, and he was barred from both Russian military
service and, years later, immigration to the United States. He had two
children in the Ukraine, Gitel and Izik. As with most of my relatives who
did not emigrate, I assume that they perished in Hitler's crematoria.

Old stories like this one always intrigued me, as did old objects and
people. In the summer I wandered sometimes through the downtown
Berkeley streets purged of college students. Even as I reveled in the bright
morning sidewalks glistening with dew, junk-store windows caught my

eye. Dusty chests, frosted-glass medicine bottles, and boxes of old photographs placed strategically near the door of an antique store invariably sucked me in, helpless, from the sidewalk; I would stumble out into the daylight hours later, dazed, seventy-five cents poorer, having perused the store's entire collection of miscellaneous photos circa 1925.

I first volunteered in a nursing home when I was 10 years old, in sixth grade. I adored the residents of the home: the wizened men bowed over the plastic trays of their wheelchairs, the three keen-eyed, murmuring matrons from whom I learned the nursing home lore, and the old blind woman who took my hand and, sighing, pressed it to her cold wrinkled cheeks.

Recently, I volunteered in a local Home for Jewish Parents with a blonde, blue-eyed friend named Jeffie. We approached a resident together, Jeffie introducing herself first. The old woman asked Jeffie to repeat her name several times; she seemed to have trouble understanding her. But when I began, "I'm Hannah," the old woman's laugh dwarfed her shrunken body. "Now that's a good Jewish name," she said, gazing at me.

And so it is … Jewish tradition maintains that the chain of life remains unbroken when babies are named after dead relatives. The relatives live on in the growing children who share their names. When those children reach adulthood and die, they pass on the names of their predecessors to a new generation. Every time I sign my name, my great-grandmother and the long line of women whose name she bore are memorialized in print. The name does not only belong to me, but to the long line of Jewish Hannahs that reaches back to the bereaved barren woman of the Torah whose woeful entreaties caused God himself to weep.

Perhaps it is because so many limbs of my family tree were severed in the European bloodbaths of the 1930s and '40s that I have adopted for myself a relatively strict code of honor. Whether I like it or not, nothing I do is for me alone, but for all of my antecedents who were named Hannah. I cannot allow myself to desecrate my name through dishonesty, cruelty, or any other means, because in so doing I debase my people.

I laid my cello down carefully on the soft low piling of the living room rug. Turning in the direction of the kitchen, I inhaled deeply, summoning the strength of my great-grandmother and her ancestors. "Mom," I said, "I'm sorry." As I exhaled, I felt the anger ebb from my body and the warm sensation of relief flood my face. I had done the right thing, I was sure of it, and I knew Hannah and Hannah, and Hannah, would have approved.

HENRY CORRIGAN-GIBBS (class of 2006) graduated from Yale University in 2010 and then worked with a research group at Yale studying ways to protect Internet privacy and anonymity. He was due to begin a PhD program in computer science at Stanford University in the fall of 2013.

It was complete and utter chaos. A sea of students stood shoulder to shoulder in a large courtyard, organized into one huge, snaking line. Teachers, many of whom looked like students themselves, scurried around frantically. It was orientation day at Berkeley High, and a thousand students were waiting to get their photos taken. There was only one camera.

I was one of the young freshmen waiting in the August heat that day, and it was my first experience with Berkeley High. I arrived twenty minutes early (to beat the crowds), brought $5 (for lunch), and figured it would take a half-hour (tops). But by the time I stepped on campus that morning, it seemed that I was the last to arrive. It became immediately clear that I certainly wasn't going to use my lunch money, seeing as I would still be at school through lunch. And, as I would soon discover, when a thousand students are involved, nothing takes a half-hour.

As the morning dragged on, the students grew restless. Water balloons sailed across the courtyard, and what began as a line devolved into an undulating mass of increasingly impatient teens. Hoping to quell the brewing riot (or not knowing what else to do), the administrators herded the entire crowd into the school's cavernous theater.

Inside the theater, the hum of post-summer conversation soon filled the stale air. Impromptu games of cards were set up in the aisles, with teachers and students camped out next to each other. All around, students introduced themselves to the people sitting close by, hoping to make a new friend and pass the time. As the lunch hour rolled by, some enterprising students made pilgrimages to the 7-Eleven, with snack orders for their friends. Eventually, a small woman appeared on the stage with a megaphone and began directing students to leave the theater and get their pictures taken. I was one of the last to be called, and left the school with my ID card just as the sun dipped below the horizon.

In the three long years since my freshman orientation, I am discovering more and more how the skills I have learned at Berkeley High have not only aided in my success at school, but also in life in general. When traveling in Cuba, my extensive experience dealing with the school administration proved helpful in dealing with the ubiquitous Cuban bureaucracy. The self-reliance the school gave me was invaluable during my summer job at a software company. (Lacking formal training, I ended up teaching myself how to do most of the job at my desk out in a storage warehouse.)

But beyond these material skills, Berkeley High has given me the benefits of an institution where the most interesting events happen by chance. Lectures about communism in government class end up with Russian immigrant students discussing the virtues of the American democratic system. The final projects of one media class evolve into a public film festival covering every topic from the death penalty to the life of the school custodian. And the freshman photo day turns into a social event for the student body. By keeping an open mind to the constant surprises offered by a large urban high school such as mine, I've been able to get more out of my time at school than I ever could have imagined.

This week, I go back to Berkeley High for my last orientation. I'm curious to find out what this year will hold.

IAN HOFFMAN (class of 2011)
attends Swarthmore College.

For my father's 44th birthday, I wrote him a poem called "Halfway." I told him that he still had plenty of time left. He didn't. He killed himself before he was 45.

I was shocked, but in truth, the signs were there. He and my mother had recently separated because he hit her. He closed his stable business to start a record company—he was full of plans. When my sisters and I visited his tiny apartment, they shared a bed and I slept on an armchair. We ate pizza off the Foosball table. I was 12, so I didn't realize that something was off. After all, for three years, my father had been depressed, and that seemed gone now. We should have known he was manic.

I remember having kind of a good time in the weeks after his death. I holed myself up in my room and played World of Warcraft. I feigned tears to skip class. For attention, I cried in front of the girl I liked. I wrote a lot. It felt good—it was my dad who first encouraged me to write. I guess it wasn't surprising that I had few friends in middle school.

In high school, for the first time, girls liked me. I was popular. I went to parties. I ditched my loyal old friends and dodged them in the halls, choosing to cling on to the "in" crowd. I stopped letting my mom into my life. For one, my behavior at parties made it impossible to do so, but I also thought talking to her wasn't "cool." I rarely thought about my father. I stopped writing. Mostly, I stopped reading. My grades fell.

Looking back, I was lost. I didn't like much about myself anymore. When I was alone—that is, without my popular friends, or without a plan to be with them—I would sometimes, accidentally, reflect. And often at these moments a crushing emptiness would descend on me. But I brushed these moments aside. It's easier to work to forget a problem than to work to solve one. I brushed them aside until my junior year. It was then that I realized I was halfway finished with high school, and I had little—little that I was proud of—to show for it.

I tried to recall what it was, so long ago, that I had liked about myself and other people. It started coming back to me. I admired the loyalty of my old friends. And so I approached them, asking for forgiveness. Many are my good friends again. I started to talk with my mom. It felt good to open up to her.

I spent time on my schoolwork again. I turned my grades around. I had stopped reading years ago, but one morning before school, I picked up *The Hours*, by Michael Cunningham. Now I read every day.

My father had always told me that I was a good writer. He used to send my poetry to all his friends, so often that it was embarrassing. I realized that I missed writing. I tried to write, but I was rusty. I wrote an eighty-page semi-autobiographical novella, but on rereading, it made no sense. I scrapped it, but I loved the act of writing. I strengthened my resolve to continue, and I worked to familiarize myself with the classics. My favorites are Joyce, Frost, Yeats, and Keats. Joyce for his brilliance; Frost for his unwavering modesty and loyalty; Yeats for his willingness to share his innermost vulnerabilities; and Keats because of my father.

A year ago, I was looking through the old bookshelf in our garage, and I stumbled on *The Collected Works of Keats*, full of my father's annotations. He liked the short poems on hope and loneliness. I like them too. My father's comments reminded me that there was so much more to him than his disease: He fundraised tirelessly for nonprofits; he traveled around the world and made friends everywhere; he was really, really, good at wrestling with my sisters and me. He taught me how to hold a fork.

I often find myself thinking of him at odd moments, like during a biology test. I think he would be proud of me, because I've taken the good things from his life. I've learned the importance of modesty, balance, and friendship, and to love reading and writing. Now, I'm no longer lost. I know where I'm going. And I'm nowhere near halfway there.

Ian Rose (class of 2005) graduated from Yale University in 2009 and is working on a PhD in geophysics at UC Berkeley's Department of Earth and Planetary Sciences.

Life is complicated; an ongoing juggling act of tasks to complete, friends to keep, sports to play, and the need to keep up in my classes. Regardless of how much I do, there is always something more hanging overhead. Every once in awhile, life's demands seem to grow far larger than is reasonable, with no solution or end in sight. That is when I go for a walk.

I live in Berkeley, directly across the bay from San Francisco. When I walk, I step outside of my home with no particular destination in mind, and if I begin early enough, no time limit. Soon I refine my direction to things like "up," or "north," or "I wonder if I can find my way to the top of that hill in the distance?" Often my wanderings lead me to Tilden, a regional park in the hills to the east. From the hillside there is a commanding view of San Francisco and much of the Bay Area. Other times I end up at the waterfront, watching people sail boats and fly kites. Sometimes I bring a book, but my destinations tend to be too windy to make much progress, so it ends up being just for show.

I enjoy these walks because they allow my mind to wander free and unfettered. So much of my time is spent doing what I need to do as a student, a teenager, or a son; these things follow me around sneakily even during my leisure time. When I walk, I bring no homework, no cellphone, and no study material. If I've chosen my destination well, it is unlikely that I will encounter anyone I know, and I will be at least a few hours away from the tasks that await me. I will have no excuse but to think about whatever I want. It is impossible to do otherwise.

Inevitably, I spend much of my time staring into the distance. I love to watch the beauty of the San Francisco skyline, the colossal cranes at the port of Oakland, and civilization as far as I can see. I love the size and shape of the skyscrapers in the distance. And I love then noting that the smallest hills dwarf the largest buildings in sight. Above all, I love the enormity of the world, and the feel for the region around my home that only a person on foot can know.

When I return home several hours later, I am often tired, but my mind is well rested and ready to re-enter the world. I still have essays to write, homework to do, practice to attend, appointments to keep, and one less day for them all. But despite this, I consider my walks to be time well spent.

JACK NICOLAUS (class of 2005) attended UCLA and moved to New York to pursue his theatrical dreams. He reports that he is a very typical young-artist-in-his-mid-20s, working as an actor and director when he is not grinding away at the day job.

My letter jacket often clashes with my leotard. I find myself quoting Shakespeare in the middle of wind sprints. When I flub a line, I have an urge to do push-ups in order to punish myself. I live in two worlds. In the theater community, I'm viewed as an enigma. Why would a smart, sensitive, talented actor partake in the macho, violent world of football?

On the football field, I'm seen as a puzzle. After all, why would a football player waste his time being introspective and artistic? I find that inside my own head these two images of myself clash, then begin to meld together, and finally combine to form the antithesis of all stereotypes. I'm a macho actor and a sensitive jock. I share my time between stage lights and stadium lights.

I have found my niche in these two different social scenes, but I see the similarities every day of my life. Juggling the pressures of being the only football-playing actor can sometimes get to me. During football season, it's hard to find time on stage. When the season is over, it's hard to keep me off it. For the past three years immediately following the season, I've helped produce and act in a completely student-run theater production, without any help from adults at my high school. Rehearsals start almost immediately, but athletes must tend to their bodies, and I manage to find time for the "voluntary" (football coach-speak for "Legally, I can't require you to come") workouts four days a week. One day sticks out in my mind particularly. I was performing the role of Big Jule in *Guys and Dolls*, for Berkeley High's musical. It just so happened that the musical was running concurrently with the football team's spring mini-camp. My coach was gracious enough to excuse me from practice when rehearsals conflicted, but on performance nights, I didn't have to be at the theater until 6 p.m. He and I saw no reason why I couldn't go to practice until 5:45 p.m. or so and then run over to the other side of campus to the theater and get ready to act.

Practice started promptly at 3:45. I am team captain, so I led the stretches. We started our calisthenics and worked up a good sweat. During the water break, I shuffled absent-mindedly through my choreography. The guys around me chuckled at my awkward movements, but I paid them no mind. Practice continued. I became swept up in the macho posturing and yelling so frequently found on a football field. By the time the clock struck 5:45 p.m., I was drenched in sweat and my adrenaline was pumping. I ran off the field and changed into my regular clothes, but since there was no time for a shower, I arrived at the theater smelling of sweat and Old Spice. I donned my costume and had my makeup applied. My muscles were beginning to stiffen up. I stretched the only way I knew how. As my cast mates did the stretches they had learned in dance class, I did my football warm-up. My cast mates chuckled at my awkward movements, but I paid them no mind. As the show approached, I helped lead the cast in a group warm-up. We could hear the theater filling up. The curtain rose, and the show began. With every scene break and wave of applause from the audience, I felt my excitement surge. When the show-stopping number hit its last note, the audience exploded. I was drenched with sweat, and my adrenaline was pumping.

JASON KATZ-BROWN (class of 2004) graduated from the Massachusetts Institute of Technology and is a software engineer. He worked at Google in Japan before returning to San Francisco, where he works at Airbnb.

My greatest disappointments and satisfactions have come from my campaign to make Linux universal. I started using Linux, an alternative free-software operating system, four years ago as my full-time operating system and fell in love with it. As I found my passion for computer science, I joined with the worldwide group of open-source software engineers to work on making Linux easy to install and use. I decided to combine my passions for computer science and the Japanese language, which I had been studying for several years in school, to encourage Japanese users to switch to Linux.

Making the programs available on Linux easier for Japanese to use was my first step. I wrote a Japanese dictionary and study tool, named Kiten, which is now shipped with all Linux distributions, which is the operating system plus selected applications that are freely available. I was excited about my contributions and on a roll.

In July 2003, I was invited by Softopia Japan, a high-tech center near Kyoto, to deliver a presentation in Japanese about open-source software development. My goal was to show businessmen how to leverage open-source development for cheaper, more reliable software. The group of about thirty high-tech executives understood what I was saying and showed interest, but I felt like proprietary software was so firmly wedged into their businesses that it would take much more than a talk from me to convince them to use Linux. They were polite, but distant from my talk; it seemed as if nothing changed, despite my best intentions and weeks of hard work.

This experience was intensely disappointing. I could see that the execs saw the future in Linux, but were daunted by the prospect of the switch from Microsoft. No matter what I had said, I did not have much power to effect change. When I thought about what was stopping them, I realized I also needed more engineering skills to design open-source solutions that would appeal to big business in Japan.

However, another opportunity arose about the same time. I figured one more way I could help Japanese Linux users was to write an improved Japanese input method for graphical Linux interfaces. I disliked not knowing what was going on when somebody types in text that magically turns into the correct Japanese characters. I wanted to understand the magic and make it work better. This was a much harder engineering task than I had faced previously, and frustration was a constant companion in the months of programming before my program actually did anything at all. But I used a modular architecture so I could skip around during development, and I enlisted the help of many online friends when I did get stuck.

Most importantly, I have made Linux easier to use, and while I haven't reached my goal of making Linux the Japanese operating system, I have made a good start. I learned a lot from this experience about how to deal with disappointment. Now I try to find stepping stones en route to my goals. I also learned to push on when things don't turn out as I hoped.

JENNIFER BURKS (class of 2004) studied at California State University, East Bay, and Gwinett Technical College in Lawrenceville, Georgia. She teaches kindergarten at the Kipp Strive Academy in Atlanta, and works with the Global Fashion Initiative (GFI), a nonprofit group that aims to build the self-worth of young women and to establish a foundation for teen mothers.

My grandma was abruptly awakened at 3 a.m. on a foggy Saturday morning. She was informed that her granddaughter was in an overnight foster home located in Sacramento, California. She was there because her mother was caught in a stolen vehicle while driving at 110 miles per hour. She rushed to the scene as quickly as possible. At that moment, I felt the system start to take over me. I went to my first foster home and went to many after that.

Being in foster care was really terrible. However, my grandmother always made it not so bad. She always kept me active and feeling as if I was just as smart and just as talented as the other children were. My grandma was my foster parent for eleven years before she passed away from lung cancer. She always encouraged me to start and complete as many goals as possible. With that strong motivation and drive, I began to look for certain activities that seemed interesting to me.

I took one step towards my goals when I joined Teens Teaching Tobacco Prevention. I started this my freshman year at Berkeley High

School, because I saw too many of my friends and family beginning to smoke, and I wanted to teach the younger children that it wasn't cool to smoke.

Echoing my passion for working with children, I began to work with the youth and children of my church. We put on programs such as musicals, pageants, and Vacation Bible school. We also went on field trips, and attended important events, including hearing motivational speakers talk about how to improve a church community. My second goal was to teach foster children that life isn't as bad as the media and society portrays it to be. I wanted them to understand that there is a whole world out there for them to learn and explore.

I have really tried to help as many foster children as I can, because I don't know how much longer I will be on this Earth, and I want everyone to know who I am. A motivational speaker once told me: "It isn't how many years you have in your life, but how much life you have in your years." Ever since I heard that saying, I have learned how to cherish every moment as if it was my last. I do now understand that I won't touch everyone, but I can reach as many foster children and youth as possible.

Despite my impediments, I have triumphed and achieved more than society ever expected of me. I am proud to be a part of the Beating the Odds Club. I know that I am a lifetime member, and unfortunately, too many children who shouldn't have to join are joining. I know that I want to go to college, however, I'm not yet sure what I want to do after college, but I know that I want to work with foster children. I have an everlasting dream to prevent as many foster children and youth from having to go into the system. That is why I have such strong determination to make a change in the world. It is up to us to make a difference in the world, because no one will do it for us.

JERMELLE NEWMAN (class of 2004) graduated from the University of San Francisco in 2008. She has worked in the biopharmaceutical industry, at Genentech, Inc., Thermo Fisher Scientific and most recently at Gilead Sciences, where she was a research associate in formulations and process development. In fall 2013, she planned to begin a post-baccalaureate pre-medical certificate program.

The most soft-hearted voice one could ever hear was my mother telling me to keep hope alive and never give up. That statement has always stuck with me and gives me confidence to succeed. I have succeeded in school. I will be the first member of my family to go to college. I am very proud about that, and I gain pride in making my family happy with my success.

I love to learn and I have pushed myself to take advanced classes that will prepare me for college. This year, I am taking three Advanced Placement courses and one Honors course. I am one of the few African-American students in those classes; for example, AP English Literature has only three black students. When I first walked through the door, all I saw were white people staring at me, probably wondering how I got into that class. I still feel like I'm in a "different world" in my classes. I feel like a visitor in a foreign land. I took the initiative to find out about the place. First, I had to go through customs (the school counselor) to get permission to go there. Then I had to get a passport (my report card) in order to get where I wanted to go. I had to speak and act a certain way, to "obey the customs." With my black peers I speak slang, because that's the way we communicate. I act more comfortable around them, because we understand each other. I have learned to communicate with the students in this new land, by expanding my vocabulary and conversation skills, by learning a new dialect.

Berkeley High School is a large urban school with incredible diversity and a wide variety of academic offerings. If one walks on campus, one will see segregation between races—students tend to associate with people of the same race. You will see me having conversations with all different kinds of people, because I believe in maximizing the opportunity to connect with people and learn from all different types of people. Now I have learned to be fluent. I learned about different cultures and how to interact in a multicultural world. At Berkeley High, there's a huge achievement gap between white students and black and Latino students. This is an enduring problem that has dampened the Berkeley community. My presence in advanced-level classes goes against the school's culture. Mostly white students take Advanced Placement courses. In the reality of Berkeley High, it's not normal for me to be in Advanced Placement courses. None of my friends who are black are in the same classes as me, and it's heartbreaking to me to notice that. I know that there are a lot of African-American students that can be in the same land, if they apply themselves like I did.

Being in a class surrounded by white students is an advantage for me because I learn about their culture and how they operate. What I learn in the classrooms, combined with my cultural background, gives me an edge. I have the best of both worlds. I am like a bridge that links two different lands together, closing the achievement gap.

JOANNA JACOBS (class of 2005) graduated from Brown University in 2009 and was due to begin her studies toward a Master's in Public Health (MPH) at Columbia University in fall 2013.

What if I'd had a "normal" sister? This is a question I constantly ask myself. My older sister was diagnosed with a brain cancer when she was 15 months old. I don't remember this because I wasn't even a fleck of an idea in my parents' minds. The doctors treated her, they did the surgery, the radiation, the chemotherapy, everything. And, in time, the tumor was gone. All that was left was a young girl with a big scar on the top of her head, the beginnings of an epilepsy disorder, and some mental disabilities. She was barely two years old, and she'd already surpassed her life expectancy.

As she grew older, and I came into the picture, her mental handicaps and her epilepsy continued to get worse. The reasons for this, I was told, were because the doctors at that time hadn't completely understood the side effects of too much radiation to the brain.

But that's all water under the bridge now, because my sister is simply the person she is. She is definitely developmentally disabled. She is definitely epileptic.

I've always been haunted by questions, wondering how my life would have been different if those cells in my sister's brain hadn't started multiplying out of control. What kind of person would I be today? The only answer I can think of is: a very different one.

Growing up around a mentally retarded person means practicing patience, all the time. I've learned to hold myself in check while waiting for my sister to form coherent sentences. I've sat holding my tongue as she takes half an hour to make a sandwich with tuna fish from a can. It is a few simple things like that that I've learned.

But what have I lost? This is the unanswerable question. I guess you can't miss what you never had, but it certainly is difficult when you have friends with older sisters. You see them receiving the hand-me-downs, having the fights, and getting the advice about boys. You see them make mistakes and learn from them. These are things I'm worried to have lost, and I blame those silly multiplying cells. It's difficult to think about.

However, I try not to dwell on the "what ifs" too much, because they hurt, and I feel alone. I've been lucky, though, because my sister is a truly wonderful and giving person. I'm not sure if she realizes all the things she's missing in life, not to mention the things I feel I'm missing.

Because of that, though, she's happy. For her, ignorance must be bliss. But for me ignorance is no option. I live with the fact that some disease, and the way it was treated, robbed me of the "normal" older sister that should have been mine.

I'm not the same person I might have been, but inevitably I am myself, created by my environment, the good and the bad. Ultimately, I believe, my sister has made me a better person.

John Stevick (class of 2008) graduated from Swarthmore College in 2012 and is working with a Bay Area real estate development firm.

There is a certain look I am greeted with upon entering a gymnasium: a cynical, unbelieving kind of look. Young men furrow their brows, unable to comprehend why somebody like me would be in a place like this. A sarcastic voice may come from a player as he gives his laces a final tug, "No-no-no, croquet practice is outside."

Laughter escapes from the others, while I keep my face straight. "I'm here for basketball."

At this point, the player's jovial tone usually turns doubtful, "To play?" More laughter follows.

"Yes, to play," I retort matter-of-factly.

The chuckling faces of the players quickly drop to disapproving glares. I turn to take out my sneakers and conceal a smile. I love the skepticism.

Basketball, for me, has always been more than a stress release or a passing seasonal sport. The intensity, the speed, the sudden drama inherent in basketball is matched by few other games. I have a restless desire to play; a tenacity that has earned me a spot on a strong varsity team. It is not that I am particularly gifted, but that I truly love to play the game. Basketball has an ineffable quality about it, a certain appeal that cannot be expressed with words, but which keeps me coming back to the gym day after day. It very well could be the power and the dexterity all wrapped up into one, or perhaps the feeling of unity when the ball moves in constant motion from player to player.

However, the aesthetics of basketball do not fully explain my dedication to the sport. The real allure of the game comes to me in other ways. It comes from the initial doubt I am forever welcomed with. I am white. And being white while playing competitive basketball in the Bay Area requires that I justify my presence and prove my skills each and every game. Opposing players immediately associate me with a small minority of players notoriously known for their limited jumping ability. I play to prove to the non-believers that I can play. My joy comes from the looks of awe as I glide past defenders and lay in a basket, when my opponent is forced to re-evaluate my abilities. I can feel the surprised acceptance emerging from what was before skepticism. The demeaning chants eventually transform into encouraging cheers. After I have established a confidence on the floor, the pressure of the game melts into enjoyment. From this shift in mentality, I begin combining fancy passes with quick cuts to set up easy scores, giving and receiving satisfactory high fives as we run back down court to set up on defense. After the game, the non-believers might shoot me a look, shake my hand, or make some gesture to inform me that their preconceived notions had been proven false. And then that one really tough critic approaches me. "Not bad for a croquet player."

I am satisfied for the moment, fully aware of the doubt and criticism I will have to face the next time around. Fortunately, I enjoy a challenge.

Joseph Shemuel (class of 2007)
graduated from Columbia University in 2011 and
is back at Berkeley High working as a health educator,
serving with the AmeriCorps program.

I was blessed with neither good handwriting nor the ability to do much of anything dexterous, at least without the aid of a keyboard and mouse. As a child, my penmanship was more quickly identified as Sanskrit or gibberish than English, and my hand-drawn artistic abilities stopped just shy of the well-proportioned stick figure. My parents had been computer users since the Kaypro, so as soon as I could sit on a lap and hold the mouse, a computer was the natural choice for me. The computer, however, wasn't initially a tool, but a way for my parents to subliminally educate me. To help me understand letters, they plugged me into games like Reader Rabbit. (Kids love alliteration, evidently.) I partially attribute my love of reading and writing to sounding out consonant blends as his bushy tail hopped from letter to letter. Reader Rabbit and I got along well at first, but I eventually decided that I had read enough inane stories about Cathy Cow and Danny Duck. It was time to start writing my own barnyard epics.

Since I first typed out "Jonah, the Happy Moose" in third grade, I haven't stopped writing. It has become a passion for me, almost an addiction. I write when I feel aggravated, relieved, overwhelmed, or just generally open, churning out several pieces a month, most of which never leave the screen. Recently, it all paid off, as I won my first writing contest and publication in a local newspaper. But none of it could happen without my computer, because over the years, my declining penmanship has made me averse to writing by hand. By granting me the simple privilege to type, my computer has been integral to my writing.

In this way, my experience with the computer has undergone a role reversal: Instead of commanding me via the words and gestures of childhood cartoons, the computer now does as I dictate with the mouse and keyboard. Instead of a crutch, it has become an invaluable resource. On a basic level, I use it to do mundane work such word processing and spreadsheets. Since I still can't draw anything recognizable with my hands, I've learned to use programs like Adobe Photoshop, which allow graphic professionals and amateurs alike to create almost any kind of two-dimensional graphic. I've designed everything from flyers for Frisbee team tryouts to graphics for the school newspaper, to a logo for a local DJ crew, The Rock-It Scientists. My art, and thus, my computer, have been as much for my friends and clients as for my own fulfillment.

But of course, my computer is not only educational and creative. It's first and foremost, as the folks at Facebook would like you to believe, intensely social. Similarly, the reputation of the computer as the anti-social geek's lovechild has disappeared; instead of insulating the user, the computer almost mandates contact with our friends, providing several different, yet simultaneous ways to interact. For some people, the method of choice is e-mail or instant messenger. For me, it's the blog, which allows me to share my political commentary and personal inclinations with hundreds of interested readers worldwide. I could go on for pages just about the Internet and the way it has revolutionized our lives.

This December, TIME Magazine chose its Person of the Year to be the ubiquitous "You." The cover featured only a computer, complete with a reflective panel for the monitor. When I picked it up off the newsstand a week ago, I saw myself staring back. This is how I often think of my computer; over the years, the monitor has been looking back at me, watching, as a boy who didn't know his ABCs turned into a young man who loved to write.

JOSHUA FRIEDMAN (class of 2012) is studying at
California State University, Los Angeles.

There's *The Brady Bunch, Married with Children*, and then there's my life—the sitcom that has not yet aired. My life is full of dysfunction and problems, but that's what keeps life interesting.

I am one of a set of premature triplets who live in Berkeley. We are 18. My brother Jeremy and I have quadriplegic spastic cerebral palsy. My other brother, Jase, does not have a physical disability, but has ADD. My parents have their own problems as well. On the bright side, if we were a TV show, we'd get great ratings.

My disability limits me in several ways. As a result of my spasticity, whenever I eat, my lap always seems to be starving and I end up with one big mess. Plus, I can't even hold a cupcake without squeezing it into pieces. I can't handwrite clearly. I can't dance. I never got to play on the monkey bars in elementary school, but that doesn't mean I didn't monkey around.

There are perks to having a disability. I'm king of musical chairs. If I ever get fat, I already have my own personal scooter. One of the more serious perks: Some people underestimate me. They think I am like a slow tortoise. This is somewhat good, because I'm able to blow their minds away in the end. Don't be fooled! No one pushes me around! I have a power chair and can drive anywhere, except drive up my parents' insurance.

Being unable to walk definitely presents challenges in life, but I learned a very important lesson in the summer of 2005 at Ability First, a wheelchair sports camp in Chico. "Where there's a wheelchair, there's a way." During the camp's one week run, coaches in wheelchairs helped me learn how to play almost every sport: golf, tennis, baseball, rugby, soccer, and track and field. I rock climbed and even water-skied, which I didn't think was possible. I went to Ability First every summer for six years, until I was too old to attend. At that camp, I experienced things I never thought I would, but that seems to be the pattern of my life.

Doctors thought I would never eat or speak, but by the fifth grade, I had spoken in front of the zoning board, and by sixth grade, I was president of the class. While others ran for president, I wheeled and won by a landside. I raised $1,000 for my grade and helped raise $200 for toys that were donated to Children's Hospital.

In eighth grade, my life took a turn for the worse. My right hip became dislocated, and I was in excruciating pain. I ended up having hip surgery in February, which meant I had to be home schooled for the rest of eighth grade. The pain did not get better, even with strong medication.

As the start of high school approached, I still carried around a knife-like pain in my hip. I transferred to Independent Studies and earned A's and B's. For tenth grade, I continued Independent Studies and took two classes at Berkeley High. Part of it is a blur because I was still on strong pain medication. However, I managed to keep my grades up. In eleventh grade, with just Motrin for pain, I attended Berkeley High full time. My grades suffered a little bit.

After school, on Mondays I participate in S.N.A.P., a disabled swim program, which I've been attending for eleven years. On Thursdays, I go to a movement school, the Avalon Academy, to help relax my body. In my spare time, I like screenwriting.

Life hasn't dealt me the best hand, but I continue to keep my poker face. I go to school and continue to keep up my good grades. My family may be crazy, but they always give me something to laugh about. I live life to its fullest.

JULIA SAELEE (class of 2006) graduated from UC Davis in 2010, and works in the accounting department of a San Francisco real estate company. She volunteers with the Iu Mien Scholarship Fund supporting Iu Mien students in higher education, and with the Lao Iu Mien Culture Association.

In my sophomore year, I experienced something that I didn't anticipate. I thought it would be a day like any other, but my mundane bus ride home would be suddenly disrupted, and my sense of identity would never again be the same.

Every day I take a one-hour ride home, and I usually enjoy it because it gives me a chance to relax after a long day at school. But on this particular day, I felt uncomfortable as soon as I took my seat. As the bus headed towards my home, I could feel people staring at me. I remember becoming angry and embarrassed as a group of boys began to make perverse and explicitly degrading remarks about girls, especially Asian girls. Since I was the only Asian girl on the bus, I knew that they were targeting me. One boy began to chant the trite *"Ching-chong"* stereotypical imitation of the Asian language. I wanted to run away at this point, but somehow I managed to stay on until I arrived at my stop. When I got home, I was at a loss about what to do, who to talk to, or how to feel. I felt ashamed and embarrassed because I was just humiliated and hadn't even defended myself.

A few weeks later, I had the chance to participate in Upward Bound's Annual Poetry Slam. My recollection of the incident on the bus still haunted me, so I decided if I wasn't able to speak up on the bus, I would now. Prior to this slam, I had never considered myself a poet, let alone imagined being a participant in a slam. The very thought of speaking in front of a large crowd was daunting. I remember shaking as I walked on stage. When I was in front of the microphone, I took a deep breath and began to tell my story. As I read each sentence, it felt as if I were redeeming myself and relieving embarrassment from the bus experience. I started out speaking slowly and calmly, but when my poem's tone changed and as I started to describe how I felt from the bus ride, I became less calm and spoke out angrily. I remember hearing my voice reverberate across the huge auditorium, piercing the silence and leaving some in the audience with a shocked expression. The sense of achievement that left me breathless that night is still with me today.

Although it was a relatively small slam, it was a supportive place to start, and I haven't stopped since then. I strive to inform others about my Mien culture through my poems and reach out to other girls who may have had similar experiences to mine and encourage them to speak out.

The following summer I participated in the same poetry slam. I was especially happy to see that I had inspired a younger friend of mine to participate also. I hope that her experience was as enriching as my own when she expressed herself in front of hundreds of people.

When I reflect back on that bus incident, I'm actually grateful that it happened. I was able to use it to my advantage and make a positive personal change. Without it, I wouldn't have started to write and perform poetry and go through an eye-opening transformation.

Now, as a senior, I can see my transformation from being that quiet and passive girl in my sophomore year to the outspoken and confident person I am now.

JULIETTE JARDIM (class of 2004) graduated from UCLA in 2008 and completed a MS in molecular biology, microbiology, and immunology from Johns Hopkins University. She is a consultant for a company in Washington, D.C., that is helping public and private medical providers digitize their records.

"*Bom dia,*" my professor says, interrupting herself, and raising an eyebrow as I rush in ten minutes late to my Portuguese class at Piedmont Adult School. "*Bom dia,*" I reply, smiling guiltily, a little out of breath and barely showered from water polo practice thirty minutes earlier in Berkeley, on the other side of the hills. I sit down in the front row and take my homework out as the teacher continues going over the difference between the verbs *ser* and *estar.* She speaks only in Portuguese, but I can follow the discussion. I'm a little more advanced than the rest of the class, which consists mainly of middle-aged men searching for some means of communication with their Brazilian girlfriends.

As I repeat, "*Eu sou americana,*" I fidget with the raggedy, knotted red strings barely hanging on my wrist. The ribbon once said *Lembrança do Senhor do Bonfim da Bahia*, which means Souvenir of Our Lord of the Good Ending of Bahia. According to tradition, if one ties the ribbon with three knots, makes a wish for each knot and then wears the ribbon until it falls off, not only will the wishes come true, but the wearer will return to Brazil someday.

It's not surprising how easily I understand Portuguese. My father is of Portuguese descent, and my parents lived in Brazil for many years. Often I hear my parents' phone conversations with their numerous Brazilian friends or my dad's Portuguese relatives. In addition, my parents speak Portuguese when they want privacy, which is incentive enough for a kid to try to understand.

My parents met while teaching at an English school in São Paulo, Brazil. Later, they and their hippie friends moved to an island off the coast of Bahia, a state in the northeast of Brazil. Throughout my life, I've heard stories of their exotic island life with fire ants, tarantulas, and snakes that they killed and ate. As a little kid, this place was both horrifying and captivating.

When I finally visited this summer, I didn't eat any snakes, but I did experience firsthand what my parents love about Brazil: an unparalleled natural beauty, a multilayered mix of African, European, and indigenous cultures, and, the best part, Brazilians' warmth and friendliness. Encouraged and inspired to interact, I pulled together my French from school and limited knowledge of Portuguese and Spanish. By the end of my seven-week stay, I could understand most conversations, and in my slow, broken, Romance language mix, I was able to communicate. I discussed Brazilian soap operas with a young couple during a layover at the airport, I taught some kids to play American card games on the beach, and I convinced a Capoeira (Brazilian martial art) student to demonstrate some of his moves. Now, on top of daily water polo practice, flute lessons, church, fall lacrosse league, and coaching girls' lacrosse, I've found time for Portuguese. I want the conversations I started in Brazil to continue. Portuguese class is almost over. "*Estar* describes what you are now, it's transitory," explains my Portuguese professor, "*Ser* is constant, something you will always be."

I think, "*Eu estou nos Estados Unidos*, but at heart, *eu sou brasileira*."

KACEY BERRY (class of 2008) was due to graduate from Bowdoin College in 2013 and was planning to spend a year on a Fulbright scholarship in Germany studying neurobiology.

My mom and I glide down the street on our bicycles. Up ahead, I can already see the pomegranates and persimmons and grapes under the many white canopies. I can already hear someone strumming his guitar and singing folk music. Already, I can smell the lentil soup and free-range chicken at the Himalayan meal stand, the fresh batches of kettle corn being packed into bags. We are at the downtown Berkeley Farmers' Market. Just as my mom and I are locking our bikes, it begins to drizzle.

Methodically, my mom sets off down the low row of tents, compiling a mental shopping list of what to get. Almost as seriously, I scour the area for the free samples. I try four types of goat cheese, three types of pear. I try a strawberry, though it's late in the season. I find mandarin oranges and tomatoes and olive oil. I sneak another sample of the orange as I run off to tell my mom that we should buy some.

Together, my mom and I buy oranges. Then, we walk to the Riverdog Farms stand, where I help her pick out golden potatoes and lettuce. As she pays for the food, I look for my friend from middle school, who works at the stand. I find him unloading boxes of produce behind the tent. He asks me whether my mom bought potatoes and lettuce again today. I smile and tell him yes.

By the time my mom and I have traveled down the rows of tents for a second time, we have chatted with several acquaintances—the parents of an old soccer teammate, the mom of one of my brother's classmates, a school board member and his wife, one of my violin teacher's students. We even ran into my uncle, who works in Sacramento on the weekdays. We now have two bags of lettuce, two dozen potatoes, almost as many oranges, and a handful of tomatoes, peppers, and apples. Our hair and clothing are slightly damp from the rain, but like the rest of the crowd, we don't mind. Just as we leave the tents, someone hands us a couple of buttons that read, "I shop at the Berkeley Farmers' Market— even in the rain!"

Berkeley is a town with a serious local, organic, "slow food" sub-culture. To some, it may seem trendy or elitist—perhaps, occasionally, it does to me, too. But in addition to wanting to support small growers who use healthy farming practices, I go to the Farmers' Market because I believe it fosters and supports a strong sense of community. It truly is a gathering place for farmers and residents from around the Bay Area, a place to connect informally with many members of my community.

LALITA KAEWSAWANG (class of 2006) came to Berkeley from Thailand when she was 13. She graduated from Wesleyan University in 2011, worked for a year as an AmeriCorps teacher in a New Orleans high school, and is now working as the New Orleans chef liaison for Dinner Lab, an underground supper club that features up-and-coming chefs at unexpected locations.

Supplementary essay for Amherst College

Many times in my life, I thought my education was over. After my younger sister was born, when I was a year old, our mother left us. Our father had a hard time finding a stable job or even knowing what he wanted to do. We were left with our grandmother, who had a business renting tricycles and a small farm where she grew bananas. She had no time for us, so we were placed in a child care boarding house from nursery school through first grade. I often sat under a tree in the child care house watching the gate to see if our grandma or our father would come to take my sister and me away.

Growing up, I heard my father and grandma argue where to get money for us to go to school. In second grade, I shyly sold candy at school to help with money, until the principal called home to say I couldn't sell at school. Well, 1,000 baht, or $25, was made toward school, and the leftover candy was mine. Later, my father found a woman and a job owning a shop selling handcrafted wood items in the north, in Chiang Mai. My sister and I moved up there with him, and I enrolled in fourth grade.

Sometimes my father and his girlfriend went out of town, and it was my responsibility to watch the shop and take care of my sister. When the dogs barked, the drunks crashed around, the wind banged on the window, no one was there for us. One experience in that shop that I will never forget was when one customer came in and ended up buying 100,000 baht, or $2,500, of furniture from me. It was hard. I had half of the prices in my head, and another half on a little piece of paper. I tried to be confident and mature. I did a good job, but it wasn't easy.

However, not very long after, my father broke up with his girlfriend, and his shop also broke down. That is when the next "stepmother" came along. She gave him a dream for a better future: his own house, new car, a new shop in Thailand, love for his children and a better education for us in the United States. I too was dreaming about what she offered and begged my father to come to America as soon as possible. His decision was made that he would send us here. The move did not turn out as she promised, but I am continuing my education.

Supplementary essay for the Common Application

At the age of 13, there was no one in my life I could trust. This was the year my father brought my younger sister and me to the United States. He stayed for a month and then went back to Thailand. We were left in Berkeley with his wife, a stepmother. She promised that we would have everything we didn't have in Thailand: a home, a mother, and love. Instead, she gradually gave us jobs to do at her restaurant. Before long, her restaurant became our home. My sister and I were forced to sleep in a dark room above the kitchen.

First, I worked for her as a favor because I thought it would pay her back for keeping us here. One day, I heard her say to her own children, "Aren't you happy? The girls are here to work for you, we just have to feed them." We ended up working seven nights a week from 5 to 11 p.m. without pay for four years. There wasn't a house or love to receive. Luckily, I was enrolled at Berkeley High School, where I found people whom I began to trust.

It took me four years to finally tell anyone about my situation. I had not wanted people to know about me before, because I really thought that without the stepmother, I would never survive in the United States.

However, my desire for liberation and education were growing. I wanted to try. In my junior year, I took a risk by sharing my story with my English teacher, Ms. W. I had just heard a college presentation from a counselor, and she had seen me cry. I didn't know then how important she would become to me, but she was the one who helped me begin to fight for my rights.

July 29, 2005, was Emancipation Day. A restraining order was served instead of our labor at 5 p.m. My sister and I left the restaurant and moved in with Ms. W. This year is my first year to get out from the hard labor that has taken away my teenage life and interest. Now, I have an opportunity to put all my attention into school, taking more challenging courses and joining Youth and Government, the Y Scholars, and leading the Language and Culture Exchange Club. I have gained my freedom and learned to trust.

Supplementary essay for Tufts University
"Education doesn't stretch your mind, if it doesn't force you to think about things in different ways…"

English is the key that changed my life. When I first came to the United States four years ago, I sat in the English classroom for English Language Learner (ELL) students and did not understand a single word. At the restaurant where I worked, I got in trouble with both customers and the stepfamily because I couldn't understand what they wanted or follow directions.

Learning English changed my perception of people. The stepmother had treated me condescendingly when I could not pronounce English words correctly, when I didn't know the meaning of the Fourth of July, or ordered wrong foods. At school, I found people who were understanding of my mistakes, helped me pronounce words correctly and learn new traditions. I realized that was a better way of treating people than my stepmother did. By my junior year, I knew enough English to tell my story in detail and to understand words from others, as if

English were my birth language. I can now communicate, share feelings and thoughts, and that is important.

Once I knew English, I knew what the stepmother did wasn't right. I gained the strength and confidence to escape from the stepmother and the initiative to fight for what I wanted to be.

LAUREN SILVERMAN (class of 2006) graduated in 2010 from the University of Michigan with a degree in political science and Latin American studies. She is a reporter and radio producer for a local Washington, D.C., area station and NPR.

In my freshman year, I was admitted into Stanford Hospital with an eating disorder.

I didn't starve myself to be thin; let's get that straight. I felt lost freshman year, I was struggling to find my niche among the other students in my school, and I turned to the only variable I felt I could control: food. I was performing a disappearing act, but at first people didn't notice I was vanishing. Looking back, it's clear I was headed in the wrong direction, but when I was caught in the middle of it, I didn't know how to get help. Finally, I told my parents I was ready to check into the hospital, and thankfully, I quickly regained my health and was released after less than a month.

As I walked outside the hospital, I embraced the fresh air along with the challenge of recovery, despite all of the statistics not in my favor. Much harder than gaining weight was the realization that I had lost friends through the whole experience, that people I met the first few months of high school might remember me as someone of whom I was not proud.

I decided to do something about my shame, to share my experience on the radio in hopes of shedding light on the misconceptions of eating disorders. Since I was an intern at Youth Radio in Berkeley, I had access to a recording studio but no idea whether some anonymous editor would broadcast my story, shoot it down, or rework it for years. I pitched my radio essay, and an editor ripped it to shreds, but I still felt compelled to write about anorexia, a subject I hadn't heard talked about from a youth's perspective on the radio before. With each digital edit I made on the computer, I wanted to go back in my life and cut out the parts I was disappointed with, to replace them with my triumphs, but I couldn't go back in time. Instead, I let my past ride the airwaves, positive that my success story would provide encouragement for others, or at least offer a voice for those too uncomfortable to share their own.

Last summer, I was awarded a Gracie Allen Award by the American Women in Radio and Television for my commentary. The organization AWRT celebrates national programming created by women. The honor meant a great deal, but more important was knowing that people were acknowledging my voice.

Two years and many revisions later, my commentary went from local radio stations to National Public Radio's "Morning Edition." Millions of people heard my personal narrative that morning, and with each person I ran into who mentioned my radio story, my shame diminished and was replaced with pride.

I didn't realize it at first, but I now see that the microphone didn't simply enlarge the sound waves of my voice; it enlarged my sense of self and obligation to my community. Long ago, the obsessive part of me left, and in the years since my recovery, I am grateful that I have learned how to turn obstacles into opportunities to grow.

Supplemental essay
Minutes after the lunch bell rang, I stepped into my first Black Student Union meeting. Only days before, I had heard the club was "open to everyone," but I soon found out that didn't mean everyone came.

A week before, there had been a brainstorming meeting with some leaders from the Black Student Union (BSU) and the editors of *The Jacket*, the Berkeley High School newspaper, on how to diversify the paper so that it could more accurately represent the student body. Many of the editors, myself included, were aware that *The Jacket* wasn't perfect, but believed it covered issues relevant to all of the students at our school. My assumptions were struck down as Rico, a classmate and leader of BSU, talked about being stopped in the halls, and the lack of college information in the black community, topics not mentioned in the paper. Rico forced me to examine my belief that my high school experience was generic, that it applied to everyone, like some sort of boring TV show. Rico had suggested some editors from *The Jacket* stop by the BSU meeting. Excited, I marked Wednesday's meeting date in my planner, but come lunchtime, no one else wanted to join me, and I kept asking myself, "Why I am doing this?" I knew I was there for more than the school newspaper; I was there to collaborate with a new group of people.

So, there I was, sticking out like a bleach stain in the dark wash, but I stayed seated. I feared that the unfamiliar faces in the BSU might call me out, as the only white person in the room, or even request I leave—but they didn't. By the end of lunch, no one had touched their food, but the whiteboard was quilted with different people's ideas for diversifying the paper. "Presenting to English classes, giving applications to different ethnic clubs on campus… " I was stunned when I raised my hand, and one of my ideas went up along with my peers' contributions.

I stayed late talking to Sherick, the president, whom I knew from soccer and dance, and with a little encouragement, I became an official member of the BSU. Looking back on this year, AP Calculus may have taxed my mind the most with derivatives and integrals, but BSU meetings opened my mind to problems unsolvable by any one formula—just the way I like it.

LAUREN SONDEREGGER (class of 2005) graduated from Yale University in 2009 and is attending UC San Francisco School of Medicine.

My favorite swimming pool has no walls, chlorine, or tile. The Golden Gate Bridge and the enclosing coastline define its limits, and Alcatraz and Angel Island are my starting blocks. This unique swimming pool is San Francisco Bay, a curiously shaped expanse of choppy teal-brown water of mysterious content, ranging in temperature from 45 to 70 degrees Fahrenheit.

As a 13-year old, I had only known competitive pool swimming. One day, a coach on my swim team enticed me to miss the first half of a grueling workout with tales of an unusual place to swim where seals might attack me, and I would reek for days after. "How intriguing," I thought, and followed my older teammates down to the Berkeley Marina for my first "Bay swim."

Since then, I've participated in this unusual sport several times a month, throughout the year, as a respite from ordinary pool swimming. Faithful to our routine, my teammates and I jump shrieking off the old, dilapidated pier at the Marina, anticipating the cold shock of the salty water and the ensuing rush of excitement and adrenaline. (I've been nicknamed "Shark-bait" because I always plunge first into the deep.) Swimming out West into the setting sun around the bayside restaurant and towards the Berkeley Pier, we battle the choppy waves and imagine in fear all the unknown creatures that lurk on the muddy floor of the Bay. We wave at the early diners in the restaurant and always get a laugh out of what they must be thinking when they see a few crazy swimmers passing by. Even after four years of swimming in this chilly water, no matter how unpleasant my day has been, or how stressed out I am, a frigid swim in the Bay has been, without fail, a great pick-me-up.

In addition to being purely for fun, our Bay adventures serve as preparation for numerous open-water races. My personal favorite is the

"Alcatraz Swim," a chilly 2,000-yard crossing from Alcatraz Island to Aquatic Park in San Francisco that I have completed ten times since I was 14. Almost 1,000 people wake up while it's still dark on a Saturday morning to board a ferry and share the anticipation of jumping into circa 58-degree water, still shrouded in fog. Whether you're wearing a two-inch-thick wetsuit as protection from the cold, or braving the elements as a "naked" swimmer like my teammates and me, everyone is proud of participating in this crazy feat. I thrive on the emphasis on the process and experience of the race. I come away from Alcatraz swims feeling inspired, refreshed, and salty, ready to tackle all that life might throw in my way. After all, I have the courage, stamina and desire to numb my extremities for the better part of an hour to do what generations of convicts could only dream of. Consequently, I am usually confident when taking an intimidating exam, and have the courage to stand by my convictions.

Another special aspect of Bay swimming for me is the connection with nature. More than once I've stopped during an Alcatraz race and looked around at the gorgeous sight of the rising sun reflecting on San Francisco. I'm overcome with the glorious feeling that I'm all alone out there in the Bay, simply because those 1,000 swimmers are hopelessly scattered on such an impressive expanse of water. I marvel at how utterly tiny I am in comparison with the enormous mass of water around me, and experience a sense of uneasiness that I love—for even though this vastness of water is my friend and teacher, it could just as easily kill me with its temperatures, tides and creatures.

Bay swimming refreshes me and brightens my day with its mix of thrill and marvelous uneasiness. To think that I sometimes pay to see creepy movies to conjure that unmistakable feeling of suspense and apprehension! More often I just go for an awesome swim in my favorite swimming pool, San Francisco Bay.

LIAM SMITH (class of 2005) graduated from Ursinus College in Pennsylvania in 2009. He has returned to the Bay Area and is still working a few days a week at Acapulco Rock and Soil.

Last summer, my father was trying to revive a bankrupt landscape supply company, Acapulco Rock and Soil. Every day, new debts would come to light, and the bookkeeper turned out to be an embezzler. The company was struggling just to keep its day-to-day operations going; but, miraculously, sales continued to be good. Summer was the busiest time, and, although my dad was reluctant to add to the payroll, the manager couldn't handle all the business by himself. He needed an assistant. After the corrupt bookkeeper, they wanted to hire someone who was trustworthy, above all. In addition, the new hire would have to be able to add in his head, and learn how to operate the computer programs, plus absorbing everything there was to know about rocks and soil. He would have to be able to sell by weight or volume, and do all of this in both Spanish and English. Not surprisingly, no one who fit this description could be found, especially at the wages they were willing to pay, so my dad asked me.

Naively, I agreed. I was excited about starting at Acapulco because it gave me an opportunity to gain real-world experience, and have a taste of the responsibilities that most people face every day.

When I arrived on my first day, I was amazed; it was only 7:45 a.m. and the yard was already buzzing. Rufino and Alfredo, the forklift operators, were loading pallets of rocks onto pick-up trucks, while landscapers patrolled the yard trying to find the perfect rock (to the trained eye, each rock really is unique, I soon learned). My job was to help the manager, J.B., keep this chaos running smoothly. Soon I was figuring out the accounting program, while trying to serve customers as quickly and competently as possible, since at this hour, they were all eager to reach their job sites. It took all of my presence of mind to enter sales correctly, identify the materials, and answer questions thrown at me by the customers, many of whom spoke only Spanish.

When the morning rush ended, I was ready for a break, but J.B. took me out into the yard for a crash course in rocks and soil. For instance, I learned not to sell people sand to put between their brick pavers, because, although it holds them together better than any other material, it washes away with the first rain. The right material for the job is finely crushed gravel called decomposed granite, or D.G. What I later learned was that D.G., like many of the materials we sold, had at least three other names in English, and a few more Spanish ones.

One of the things J.B. liked about me was that I was able to retain this kind of information, and he only had to tell me things once. By the third day, I knew enough about the products and I could work the computer well enough for J.B. to leave me to run the business by myself while he got lunch.

At first it was nerve-wracking to be on my own. But after I was able to resolve problem after problem by myself, I became confident in my ability to handle just about anything that could come up, even if I had to improvise. By the end of summer, I was working full shifts as manager by myself. I have always had an ability to think on my feet, but after my time at Acapulco, I feel that I have the confidence to apply this ability in chaotic and intimidating situations that might have scared me before. I believe this quality will help me make the best use of the intellectual training that I hope to acquire, and will stand me in good stead both at college and in the world beyond it.

LYLA KELLEY (class of 2013)
planned to attend McGill University.

The Eastern Sierras have been a part of my family for over fifty years, beginning when my grandfather, Pop, abruptly bought a gold mine in a small valley next to Mono Lake called Rattlesnake Gulch. His stone mining cabin with a tin roof is still there today, serving as a monument to Pop.

Only an extraordinary and eccentric man like my grandfather would claim a gold mine on a whim. It was not a "get rich quick" scheme. He simply liked dynamite, the outdoors, and solitude. A few trees, sagebrush everywhere, majestic granite rocks 150 feet high, minty leaves emitting a cool, sweet fragrance that tickles the nose, and antique gun shells and tin cans sporadically strewn about the gulch was a paradise for Pop.

Pop lived at Rattlesnake Gulch for years. His life in the Gulch complemented his fearless eccentricity. One summer, no surprise, we discovered a rattlesnake in the main camping area, close to young kids. Pop quietly walked into his cabin, came out carrying a pistol, shot the rattlesnake in the head and casually returned to the stone house. On a different occasion, Pop decided he wanted to blow up a boulder. He bought a large amount of dynamite (without telling anyone) and left what he didn't use in his cabin. After he died, we discovered it in a casserole pan. We had to bring in the Navy SEALs to blow it up.

Like my grandfather, I have a deep love and respect for nature. As soon as I take my first steps in the Gulch, I smell the cool sage and remember that the Eastern Sierras are more significant than anything back in Berkeley. I can imagine Pop feeling the same way. However, unlike my grandfather, I am comfortable with people. He moved to the mine to get away from everyone, but I never find myself trying to escape others. Throughout my childhood and adolescence, I have befriended ostracized kids when no one else would. One of my closest teammates was a

girl named Emma. She was intensely competitive, which scared and an-
noyed the other girls. But I looked beyond her thirst for winning and saw
a sweet and passionate girl who shared my love for gymnastics. I never
tried to change her. Pop did not have the flexibility to understand these
ostracized kids, because he himself was similar to them. It was easy for
him to go away because he felt he didn't belong. My empathy lets me acknowledge people like Pop, when most do not.

When I bring friends to the mine, I enjoy watching the blank looks
on their faces when we first arrive. To them, there is nothing there, nothing significant or beautiful about Rattlesnake Gulch. I chuckle. I know the
truth. Behind their initial impressions, there is extraordinary life.

I embrace the beauty of the mine, and being exposed to this raw
environment made me accepting of the eccentric. I will have infinite
opportunities if I simply leave my mind open.

MARCELO BOURQUE PEREZ (class of 2013) was a member of Berkeley
High's acclaimed Jazz Combo A, which was named High
School Combo of the Year by *Downbeat* magazine.
He planned to attend the University of Miami.

Screams echoed through my house. It was freshman year, and my
mother and I were fighting. As she tried to make a point, she mispro-
nounced a word. I was so caught up in the moment that I lost all good
judgment. "You are such an immigrant, you can't even pronounce the
word right," I screamed. I immediately realized that I had made a huge
mistake. I was scared, confused, and saddened that I had hurt the most
important person in my life.

While my mother and I are both Latino, our lives are very different.
After escaping the civil war in El Salvador, my mother went to high

school in a predominantly Latino area in Los Angeles. Luckily, being successful did not separate her from her culture. At Berkeley High School, academic performance divides us students by race. In general, at our school, people of color excel less than Caucasians, and the segregation in the classroom usually extends into our social groups. This environment made me feel obligated to choose between success and culture. Despite my mother's best efforts to ensure my strong Latino identity, I chose "success." Over time, even though I felt great about my academic and musical achievements, distancing myself from my culture made me feel invisible. I was deeply conflicted.

The summer of my junior year I traveled to Havana, Cuba, with the Berkeley High Jazz Ensemble to study music. Being Latino and fluent in Spanish gave me the ability to connect with Cuban people across political and economic divisions. But music allowed us to understand each other intimately. I had the privilege to play with Cuban musicians away from the rest of my group. Playing music in an all-Latino environment was a life-changing experience. Music brought me closer to my heritage than ever before. It was then that I realized that my academic and musical success didn't have to isolate me from my culture. I did not have to choose between achievement and my identity.

Reflecting back on the argument I had with my mother, I see how far I had grown from her and my community. I realized the insult was not only offensive to her, but to myself. I am as Latino as my mother is. I grew up eating *pupusas* and *pozole*, I grew up speaking Spanish, and I was sung "*Las Mañanitas*" on my birthdays, just as she was. My experience in Cuba helped me reconcile all the things that define me, and made me want to grow closer to my Latino self.

Now all I have to do to reconnect with my Latino culture is recall marching down Market Street in San Francisco, chanting "*El pueblo unido jamas sera vencido*," surrounded by a sea of beautiful brown people. Memories like this one, when I am completely immersed in my culture, fill me with love, pride, and appreciation for this part of me. I am no longer lost. I will always cherish the totality of who I am.

MARVEL WILSON (class of 2010) is a student at the Polytechnic Institute of New York University.

"You know the 57 stopped going to Bayfair?" I couldn't believe it when I heard it. The 57 bus line represents my whole life's journey. From San Leandro, playing tackle football on cement, running away with Monopoly money; to the 100s (Avenues) in Oakland, where I learned the meaning of ghetto gospel and "I am my brother's keeper," then all the way to Rand Avenue, when I became a lake boy. The 57 had a lot of firsts for me—my first time riding the bus by myself, my first fight, my first love, and my first break-up. The 57 is one of the few buses that travels through all of Oakland; it crosses community boundaries and physically manifests the mobility of each of the diverse groups.

On any given morning, you can find students going to Fremont High, Oakland Technical High School, or Oakland High School. The dozens of Asian students up front muffling their laughs; the shy girls with gel-less ponytails and their textbooks pressed against their chest sitting in the middle; and of course the "hyphy" culture dominating the back: boys in black hoodies despite the 80-degree weather and bold girls laughing loudly while their multi-colored braids bounce behind them. An hour earlier, the 57 would have been stuffed to the brim with migrant workers leaving and entering the Fruitvale district in search of work. Their gray shirts full of holes and faded tight jeans hold an odor of hard work and cheap paint so pungent it seems to mock the pre-osteoporosis fingers of wives and girlfriends who tirelessly try to wash the scent away. The tardiest riders of the morning are the

30-something year olds who purposely ride late to avoid the music-blasting, foul-mouthed teenage crowd.

Those images of the 57 are some of the first thoughts that come to mind when I think about how I grew up. My household was a place of one-track thinking, unchallenged and unchanging. Those bus rides helped me understand that life and knowledge are varied and multi-layered, and it made me thirst for more experiences and points of view. That thirst has remained intact throughout my academic career. In learning, I investigate and present as many different sides of a topic as I can. Challenging traditional or common constructs is what keeps me interested and deepens my understanding. Above all, the 57 showed me that wisdom and knowledge are interconnected, but the connection has to be sought to be seen and grasped. For example, composite functions with frequently changing rates is a concept I struggled with in Calculus until I studied gerrymandering in U.S. Government class. I would break apart the functions in a way that kept me from finding the variable I was looking for. Learning how politicians used changing variables to their advantage in redistricting enabled me to handle the formulas. I set them up so that whatever piece of the function I was looking for (be it the rate of change of an oil spill or the area of a basketball as it fills) was tweaked to get the result I wanted. And this epiphany is no different than another: after having misbuttoned my shirt and defended my fashion gaffe to a room full of people, I realized that cool is just a state of mind.

At 5:30 in the afternoon, and the day turns from a bright excess of primary colors to a dingy and monotonous gray. Despite this, I inhale deeply because the symbol of the end of the day has come into view. I succumb to the desire of smiling and straighten my posture. The thrill of the unknown excites me and the familiarity gives me confidence, the vessel that has coached me to be critical, quick-thinking, worldly, and empathetic got me on track to achieve what I want. It also makes sure no matter where I go that I return home. The 57 drove me from my beginnings and I found my own way toward the future, I just hope that as the 57 rolls on, it enjoys the ride as much as I do.

MELEIA WILLIS-STARBUCK (class of 2003) completed two years at Dartmouth College before she was tragically shot and killed on a Berkeley street in the summer of 2005. At the time she was working in a women's shelter.

I slid my nails across the speckled table and down the leg. My fingernails tapped against the cold metal as I sat in my seventh-period chemistry class waiting for the first bell to ring. My eyes rolled towards the clock. The minute hand, after what seemed like hours, finally reached the six. *Briiiiiiiiiiing*. Once the rest of the class settled, our teacher rose from his chair. After removing his hands from his pockets, he proceeded to speak. "Welcome to the first day of the second semester. I'm sure you all have noticed that we have lost a few of our students." Half of the class was missing, to be exact. The students who had failed consisted of all the minorities, with the exception of myself and a few Asian students. "It's unfortunate, but a lot of them just couldn't cut it. After all, they earned the grades they received." He continued to talk to the class about our lost group of students, but I forced myself to stop listening.

A high failure rate for minorities is one of the many effects of the achievement gap that Berkeley High School is so famously known for. Traces of the achievement gap can be found in places other than the classroom. When lunch is over and the first bell rings, signaling to everyone to return to class, all the white students pack up their belongings and walk towards their classes, while black and brown students continue to mingle amongst their peers.

Although I have a diverse group of friends, my immediate social circle is predominantly black. Like the majority of African American students at Berkeley High, they too don't attend class regularly or on time. Forcing myself not to hang out with my associates after lunch has ended and fourth period has begun requires a lot of willpower. As a result, I have been forced to learn at an early age that it is important to surround myself with those who succeed, and sometimes this means leaving people behind.

However, constantly succeeding without my black and brown friends is far from a solution. I have decided that I am going to take a more pro-active stance on this problem, which has been plaguing Berkeley High for a number of decades. I am well known for my involvement in many campus organizations and extracurricular activities. I have used this to my advantage. Whether I'm fulfilling my role as the Black Student Union president, a peer health educator, or the president of the Honor Society, I bring awareness to achievement gap-related issues.

During my sophomore year I served as a member of the board of directors for a youth-run organization titled African American Latino Leadership (AALL). We began to tackle achievement gap-related is-sues that the Berkeley School Board hadn't even begun to discuss. We created mentor groups, provided tutoring, and hosted events that con-nected minority families. For all this awareness, however, I have yet to devise an effective and appropriate way to confront the snide remarks of a teacher proud to have gotten rid of the minority students in his class. I plan on working on it during the remainder of my education.

MOLLIE SCHOENWALD (class of 2005) graduated from Northwestern University and now works at Coach in New York, where she manages store planning and allocation for all 350 free-standing stores in North America.

I tentatively opened the door to Room C113 on the first day of my freshman year, to be greeted by Mrs. Karla Herndon, whose unassuming paisley sundress and calm demeanor was merely a show for the freshmen, she made sure to tell us. Majestically perched on her rickety stool, hands folded in her lap, she suddenly burst into song: "*Eram, eras, erat, eramus, eratis, erant,*" to the tune of "The Mexican Hat Dance." Soon the entire class put aside their nervousness and joined her in singing. Already I knew that she was no ordinary teacher.

C113 was my escape from the pandemonium of Berkeley High School. There, Mrs. Herndon gave us the key that revealed the buried world of Virgil, Caesar, Livy, Cicero, and Ovid, and made it come alive. As we gazed up at Mrs. Herndon during her lectures, I could hear the bustle of senators rushing through the Forum, I could discern Cicero standing at the Rostra declaring the guilt of audacious Catiline, I could sense the tension of a country on the brink of civil war. She led me far beyond the fourth declension or the passive periphrastic; she led me into the daily lives of the Roman people—their architecture, culture, habits, and literature.

I did not fully understand where Mrs. Herndon was guiding me until one foggy day in February of my junior year. With the smell of Mrs. Herndon's cauliflower lunch still lingering in the air, the Latin class trickled into C113. Some excited, some lethargic, we sat down to translate the *Aeneid*. My revelation came as we read the passage in which Aeneas and his comrades encounter a ferocious storm at sea. Mrs. Herndon lectured on timelessness, on the immortality of Virgil's characters, on the larger-than-life situations, on the moral lessons contained in the text, which have as much relevance today as in Virgil's time. From beneath her lovingly worn text, she pulled out a letter written by her father during his service on a battleship in World War II. As she read this letter, her voice never faltered: Instead, her intensity heightened with every crashing wave and pounding surf—emotions and scenes depicted exactly like those that we had translated only minutes before. It clicked. The parallels of the two storm scenes blossomed in my mind, recalling the disregard for human life during times of war. Even more broadly, I saw the connection between the *Aeneid* and modern struggles, both national and personal. This realization of historical continuity overwhelmed me. At that moment, I knew my fate as a classics major had been sealed: *Iacta alea est*, the die has been cast.

MOLLY STEWART-COHN (class of 2004) graduated from Vassar College in 2008 and works as a freelance theater lighting designer and technician in the Bay Area.

The tradition in the theater department of my school is to allow the technical staff to take a bow on closing night. After the actors have gone through the motions of curtain call, the techies file onstage, hands linked, to make our bow, before stepping upstage. I always downplay the importance that taking the bow has to me (after all, what would a true techie care about being seen on stage?) yet in reality, this brief interlude in the otherwise actor-reserved space is one of the highlights of any school show.

Why I feel this way is a mystery. I certainly don't desire to be an actor; I have a long list of reasons why I find technical work preferable. The stage itself is not an unknown territory. I do a large amount of work on it, whether it be focusing lights or repairing cables or moving sets into place. Yet when the house is filled with people, their faces indistinguishable but obviously turned in your direction, the uncomfortably warm lights shining in your eyes, the stage is suddenly a different realm, one normally left exclusively for the actors.

Perhaps I have some buried dramatic spark that urges me towards performance, nourished by my theatrical family and a childhood of Shakespeare plays and Broadway musicals, which lends me a fondness for extravagant hand gestures or prompts me to make flamboyant bows after performing scene changes, even though nobody can see me. More likely, I simply relish the acknowledgment of my work that a closing night bow gives me. For weeks, the technicians work behind the scenes, devote their lunchtimes to building scenery, and come in extra days to focus lights so that the first day actors arrive at the theater, everything is, almost magically, ready for them. On closing night, actors step aside for a moment to let the techies take center stage, and, for once, the audience sees evidence of the invisible people responsible for all the little theatrical miracles, the lights and sounds and sets, that transform a show from a bunch of teenagers reciting memorized lines to a real place and story the audience can get lost in. After all my hard work, I get to leave my post, walk onstage, and receive a moment of clapping and a word of thanks.

This year, I've been promoted to co-head of the tech crew and lighting designer. Consequently, I've spent the last few weeks holding one-sided conversations with my friends about the merits of purple light over green. I've been indulging the overly organized, mathematical side of my personality by fantasizing about how to logically arrange the other techies to most efficiently hang and focus the lights. I relish the opportunity to run the crew in a more professional, coordinated way than before, when nobody really had an assigned task. Yet, secretly, I look forward to closing night, when I will not only get to bow, but will be acknowledged for the first time by name, and I'll step forward to receive a bouquet of flowers.

MORANDON HENRY (class of 2013) planned to
attend Oral Roberts University in Oklahoma.

What to say? What not to say? Should I be transparent or should I keep
my personal trials and life's lessons to myself? Should I reach out and
help? Or should I just stand on the sideline and hope everything turns
out all right? I think we all are faced with these personal questions.

We must remember there's a whole generation waiting to hear our
stories. They are waiting to hear us tell them when to say "no" and how
to say "yes."

Being the son of two youth advocates, I see children who are in
need of someone to love them enough to pour out a little of themselves
and share a little time, and just simply show that they care. I've seen
children come into our home who were just in love with the fact that my
Mom took time to teach them how to cook and properly serve a home-
cooked meal. They sat in amazement when my Dad volunteered to teach
them how to drive and how tune up their own car someday. And at the
end of the day, before these children would go home, I would hear the
same statement: "You guys are lucky; I wish I could live here!"

We've never had a lot of money, and to be honest, this quest for a
higher education will definitely be a tough one financially for my parents,
considering I'm the fourth of five children, with my three older siblings
in college as well. But I still believe in spite of the obstacles, I will always
come out on top, because someone loved me enough to share the one
thing that is worth its weight in gold: They shared their time.

The time my pastor took to teach me "The fear of God is the beginning of wisdom." The time my grandmother takes on holidays to walk
around the dinner table and send prayers to God for our protection and
his unmerited favor over our lives. The time my kindergarten teacher
took to share with the students' parents innovative ways to teach us how
to read and learn more effectively. The time our president of the United

States, Barack Obama, took to make wise choices as a young man so he could someday win the presidency and show a perfect example of strength and perseverance. I applaud all these people for sharing with their lips as well as their deeds.

At Berkeley High School, where I serve as BSU President and ASB Treasurer, we cook and serve an annual Christmas dinner for one of the city shelters. A gentleman standing in line last year began to talk to me as I stood at the door to greet each guest. He asked me about my plans after high school. I shared my goals for the next six years with him. Before he took his seat, he challenged me to find him when I graduate and start my new career. He said that he simply would like to know; how I made it? I was changed at that very moment and realized that I may not be able to find this same man in about five to six years, but he was making the point that I should remember our conversation and come back to my neighborhood and share words of wisdom with another young person who may want to go to college, who may feel afraid, not smart enough, rich enough, or good enough to complete college and live a fulfilling life.

I will complete my degree in tribute to two wonderful, hard-working parents who only give me their very best, my four siblings, who have more faith in my abilities than I deserve, and my community, which will always need a helping hand. In six years, I will remember my past and make a contribution to a brighter future of other young people by sharing something that means the most, my time.

MORGAN ROSE (class of 2013)
planned to attend UCLA.

"Hey, guys, you want to learn more about female empowerment?"

I speak confidently and with a smile, looking out across the plastic picnic table strewn with neon flyers and chocolate kisses. It is freshman orientation at Berkeley High School, and I am representing my club, the *Vagina Monologues*. With my booth wedged between the Reading Club, the Roman Re-enactment Club, and the Crew Team, it's an understatement to say that my poster —which reads "Vaginas Unite!" in glittering pink letters—stands out. A group of overconfident 14-year-old boys snicker at my opening line. Most attempt to saunter past my booth, but one slows and gives my table a second look. Looking at him directly, not wavering as his eyes dart nervously towards the sparkling letters, I ask if he has heard of *The Vagina Monologues* before.

"No," he responds, eyeing his friends who are begrudgingly waiting. Knowing that my time is limited, I launch into my speech.

I begin by telling him how *The Vagina Monologues* is part of an international organization called "V-Day" that raises funds and awareness for female victims of violence and sexual abuse worldwide. I explain how only women are allowed to audition for the show, but how men are encouraged to help with educating the student body about these issues. I relate how the show unites a multicultural group of young women within our complex school community. I describe how it gives women hope and how Berkeley High raised thousands of dollars for women's charities last year. Though he looks a little unsure, he keeps listening.

Despite having grown up in one of the most diverse, progressive cities in the world, I still see cultural taboos surrounding women's issues everywhere. As I sit at my picnic table, I watch parents either laugh condescendingly or do a double-take at the sight of the word "vagina." But these incidents don't dishearten me: They make me more determined.

Addressing women's rights as a teenager has allowed me to strive for global acceptance and sensitivity. I have learned to view those who are ignorant or uneducated about female advocacy as people with untapped potential to learn and evolve. And even if it is just the mindset of one, awkward 14-year old boy, I know that I am changing minds and lives.

"Putting your e-mail address down just lets you stay informed about women's rights events on campus," I say. "And yes, you can totally take a piece of chocolate." "All right!" he says enthusiastically, and jotting his e-mail down on the list, he grabs a Hershey's kiss and triumphantly quips "Free candy!" to his friends as he rejoins them. They all chuckle and slap him on the back. But as they glance back at my table while walking away, I know that they heard me.

NAOMI FA-KAJI (class of 2009) enrolled at Rice University after a gap year. She will graduate in 2014.

"You put your right hand in ..."

I belted out across the courtyard, thrusting my arm in front of me. One hundred twenty pairs of wide brown eyes followed my every movement.

"You put your right hand out ..."

Some of the older children sang along, but the majority of them just laughed, following the crazy American leading them in this song.

"You put your right hand in and you shake it all about."

One hundred twenty hands flapped about wildly (though I suspected that the majority of them were not right hands).

"You do the hokey pokey and you turn yourself around ..."

My voice was going hoarse as I spun dizzily in a circle, waving my hands around above my head. Then a swelling of sound as 120 voices joined in for the line they all knew:

"That's what it's all about!"

Growing up in Berkeley, California, I have seen almost everything on a bumper sticker. Tirades against conformity ("Friends Don't Let Friends Drink Starbucks"), fanciful expressions ("I Brake for Elves"), ironic catchphrases ("My Karma Ran Over Your Dogma"), quotes both inspirational ("Do or Do Not, There Is No Try—Yoda") and mundane ("I Heart My Cat"), views on political issues ("Animals Are Little People in Fur Coats"), pride in personal characteristics ("Dyslexics Have More Fnu!")—you name it, it's out there. One day, I noticed a bumper whose owner mused: *What if the hokey-pokey really is what it's all about?*

Last July, I headed to a village outside of Chennai, India, as one of only two teenagers in a small group of volunteers. We worked in an orphanage founded by an Indian American woman, originally from Chennai herself. Forty-one children live at the orphanage—survivors of hard street life, abandonment as infants, and abuse. The orphans have known hunger and great tragedy. All have lost at least one parent to accidents, cancer, suicide, or AIDS. Meeting the founder in Oakland and hearing the stories of these children inspired me to raise money in order to work and live with them for the summer.

The children at the orphanage attend the local public school, where the other volunteers and I taught English each day. The future of the children living in the surrounding villages is unclear. Many will begin working after completing the sixth grade. Yet, even though these children were the poorest of the poor, they would run out to meet us as we walked from the orphanage to the school each day, enthusiastically bestowing us with flowers and candy.

I arrived in India after an overly stressful junior year. I had been sick on and off for most of the second semester and was thoroughly fed up with classes, tests, and learning in general. I was struggling to remember moments of pure discovery—times when learning had held excitement for me, untainted by worries about grades. When I learned that I would be helping to teach English, I was apprehensive. I imagined that, once the novelty of having an American teacher wore off, I would have to fight to keep my students interested in our simple curriculum and "fun" songs.

I discovered that my hesitation was unfounded. School wasn't something to be dreaded. When I expressed sympathy for a girl who told me about an upcoming math exam, she corrected me, "No, Auntie. Exam is good. Is fun." On many occasions, while I was planting trees with the other volunteers at the orphanage, the kids would return home from school. They would eagerly crowd around us, taking up shovels, digging beside us. If there was nothing that needed to be done, they would still go around excavating random clumps of crabgrass until the whole compound was pockmarked with patches of churned soil. When they found me washing their clothes by hand, the older children would join me in scrubbing, whacking the laundry with exuberance to get the excess water out. The younger children proudly carried the clean clothes to be hung up, a long row of colorful flags dancing in the wind. To them, there was no line between work and play.

Though the children delighted in all of the songs we taught them, "The Hokey Pokey" was by far their favorite. It was simple and silly, and every group of kids wanted to sing it. Each day, after teaching reading and writing to six grades, we took the whole school outside and performed the song together. With each rendition, I began to shed my pessimism and to rejoice in simple things that money can't buy—the thrill of learning and the joy of living in the moment.

As I stood in the circle and thought, "Man, aren't we a sight?" I answered myself, "Who cares?"

That's what it's all about!

NATHANIEL SMITH (class of 2005) graduated from
Dartmouth College in 2009 and is working in marketing
for a Bay Area solar energy firm.

My Saturday mornings have always been spent in bed with a book,
most likely one I fell asleep reading the night before. All of my life, what
I've read has made an impression on me. Books have given me the key
to experience the world as I do. One thread has been a love of the sea
and the heroes that come with it.

I received the *Hornblower* series in the second grade; true, my
mother read the books to me. I followed Captain Hornblower with the
Howard Pease series—tramp steamers, third mate Todd Moran, mysteries in the depths of the South Pacific, and the fog-shrouded wharves
of Depression-era San Francisco. Then came 23 books in the Alexan-
der Kent *Bolitho* series, following Richard Bolitho in the British Navy
through the American Revolution and the Napoleonic Wars. I realized
all these early heroes of mine believed one thing: "Life is an adventure—
say yes to it, and see where you go."

And they were right. Following this heroic thread in my own life,
I can trace learning to sail in elementary school as part of a flotilla of
dinghies braving the elements of the San Francisco Bay, to competing in
my Laser off the coast of San Diego, to a Naval Academy summer semi-
nar living the life of a plebe (to the puzzlement of my Berkeley friends),
and finally, this summer, a forty-day Outward Bound tall ship sailing
course climbing the mast to furl sails, standing watch all hours, navigat-
ing amongst commercial shipping, and diving into the frigid waters of
Nova Scotia for Outward Bound's dual swim test and bathing session.

Just as my heroes promised, while I sailed the northern Atlantic
I met adventure. Hit with an attack of appendicitis, I was helped by
sailors of the French Coast Guard to balance and jump from ship to
ship in a rainstorm, where a volunteer French doctor holding a rusty
knife greeted me by mimicking surgery—his idea of a joke. The Coas-

ties took me to Saint-Pierre et Miquelon, a small French island off the Newfoundland coast, where I spent the night undergoing an emergency appendectomy. Under the influence of morphine, I found I was fluent in French, which was fortunate, as no one spoke English. It was a one-telephone hospital, which I used to have money wired to me so I could pay for the fine services of the island surgeon and to purchase passage on a small plane that flew out twice a week. I spent four days in that hospital listening to the whispers in French, "*C'est le type du bateau*"— the guy from the boat. After being discharged I flew to St. John's, where I met the ship that left me stranded five days earlier. The ship, however, sailed on without me, and I was left to experience my Outward Bound solo in a Maritime hotel—complete with room service—while I recovered from the operation. As I hobbled around St. John's, tender of stomach, I kept in mind how my heroes would have handled themselves: with courage and good cheer. With that in mind, I set off to find a good bookstore.

NIA LAZARUS (class of 2012) is a student at Georgetown University in Washington, D.C.

I am fluent in English, American Sign Language, and Latin. I am also studying Italian, and I must say I am *molta brava* at it! My love for languages and intellectual challenges led me to leave the comfort zone of the California School for the Deaf (CSD) in Fremont for the hectic halls of Berkeley High. At CSD, I enjoyed the cultural connection and ease of chatting with teachers and close friends—as quick as our hands could move—but the opportunity to study Latin and participate in Berkeley High's International Baccalaureate program was irresistible.

My interest in languages was instilled by my sixth-grade English teacher, Ms. Yoshitake, who introduced me to etymology through short lessons of Greek and Latin root words. It was mind-blowing to learn that the words "nullify," "annul," and "annihilate" were all derivatives of the Latin words *nullus* and *nihil*, meaning "nothing." That knowledge ignited a burning desire in me to take Latin courses in high school. Not realizing how often I had talked about studying Latin ad nauseam, one evening my dad surprised me with a Latin study book. To my mother's dismay, I stayed up late many nights with a camping flashlight strapped to my forehead absorbing the words in this book, although the abla-tive case and the gerund made no sense to me at the time. Later, I came across several German words in various movies and decided to self-study this language. I found its resemblance to English very *kühle*. Dur-ing my spare time, you would catch me furiously scribbling German personal pronouns, verb conjugations, and sentence structures in my plastic sky-blue composition notebook. My fascination to dive deeper into languages continued to evolve as I transitioned from German to the Romance languages: Italian, Spanish, and French. To this day, I still reference the same composition book as a study guide. Although I am Deaf I intend to become fluent in as many languages as possible.

Here is how I learn as a Deaf student. Mr. Rodrigues is teaching my class about the Truman Doctrine, and I find the Cold War an interest-ing topic. I am a bit tired after lunch and would like to rest my eyes while simultaneously listening to the lecture—like Olivia, who is sitting to my left. But I can't. I focus on the teacher's facial expressions while reading his lips and quickly shifting my attention to my American Sign Language interpreter, precisely paralleling the interpreted information with the manner in which the teacher conveys it. It sounds like a stren-uous task, but thankfully, it is second nature to me, as I have been using interpreters in classroom settings since the age of two.

Not only am I a student who studies hard at Berkeley High, I am also an athlete. I was one of four African-American rowers on the crew team during my freshman year and certainly the only Deaf one. I understood everything the coxswain said because I had taught her the signs necessary to keep me in sync with the other rowers. My sophomore year, I decided to try out for volleyball and made the team. I have grown to love volleyball and was interviewed on the Cal-Hi Sports newscast, which aired in November 2010. Last week, I sat in the bleachers with my teammates working on homework while waiting for the Junior Varsity team to complete their game. Behind me, five feet away, a teammate lightly stomped on the bench I was sitting on to get my attention, and I instantly looked up at her. She informed me that it was time to get suited up for the varsity game. My crew and volleyball teammates experienced working side by side with a Deaf person and I was able to show, and hopefully leave them, with a lasting impression that Deaf people are not dysfunctional. As a Deaf person, I think I am quite *impressionante*!

NINA GORDON-KIRSCH (class of 2007) graduated from the University of Southern California and is on a Fulbright scholarship in Israel studying water quality.

I believe practicing social justice does not preclude having a good time. I do a variety of volunteer work, but my favorite "make a difference" activity has been the clothes swaps that I organized and implemented.

After the Asian tsunami of 2004, I set out to run a clothing drive and realized I could make it an opportunity to socialize as well as provide help to the victims. As a girl of action, I typed up flyers and handed them out at school. The flyers drew more than thirty girls to my house carrying bags of clothes: jeans, fancy dresses, tank tops, T-shirts, sweatshirts, and shoes. Girl after girl came through my front door, helped themselves to refreshments, and proceeded to try on clothes. I instructed each donor to keep five items, and then we folded the rest into twenty large brown boxes. The swap was such a huge success that I decided to make it an annual event.

Over the years, I've donated to the tsunami, poor children in Brazil, and Katrina Relief. However, this fall, I wanted to help out in my local community, so I brought the clothes to the Youth Emergency Assistance Hostel (YEAH), a youth shelter in Berkeley.

NOAH FINE NATHEL (class of 2005) graduated from Cornell University and is working on his PhD in organic chemistry at UCLA.

My family loves food. When we're not eating, we're talking about eating. My parents always fed me relatively healthy foods (with the occasional Oreo thrown in). I ate whatever was there, and never thought much about it. Then I learned intriguing information about nutrition and health, and nothing has been the same for me since.

For example: Certain porous fruits soak up pesticides to a concentration that is dangerous. Strawberries and peanuts are profoundly affected. So, unless the strawberries and peanuts were grown organically, that good old PB&J—lovingly packed off to school as a "healthy lunch"—is anything but healthy. Call me weird but, when I was 14, the irony of this had me spellbound.

My interest in health started even earlier. When I was 11, I picked up a children's book about diseases. I remember that its tone was perversely cheery. The diseases were alphabetized, and I quickly became engaged in the section on cancer (Look under "C"!), no doubt experiencing a touch of hypochondriasis (Look under "H"!). Later, in biology class, I became enthralled with the genetic process, and how the smallest aberration could result in a life-threatening disease.

After the strawberry-peanut epiphany, I began to pay closer attention to ingredient labels—but recognized that I wasn't exactly living the healthiest lifestyle. Like many kids, I'm massively sleep-deprived. When I'm wiped out after an all-nighter, it wouldn't matter whether my diet were certified organic or comprised entirely of Snickers and Mountain Dew. I've addressed this common problem by starting an Insomnia Club at school (where kids can learn about the importance of sleep, and even catch a wink during meetings). Nutrition is vital, but so is a healthy lifestyle.

I want a broad undergraduate education, but I'd definitely like to do some disease-related research in college—something like Professor Judah Folkman's work on angiogenesis inhibitors that starve tumors of blood they need to grow, or maybe even something of my own on the nutrition-lifestyle-cancer connection. After college, I want to go to medical school and then specialize in oncology. Like many people considering a medical career, I've been wondering how I'll handle the emotional part of working with real patients. So I became a volunteer at a home for terminally ill children. At first, the facility seemed like Eden. I read the popular children's story *Frog and Toad* to a young patient there. Then I got an e-mail from the administrator that she had died.

I've learned facts and empirical data about diet and lifestyle issues that inspire me and that have led me to make changes to improve my health. I know how fortunate I am to have so many compelling learning opportunities ahead of me. I relish my luck, and become even more earnest about practicing oncology whenever I remember the irony of reading *Frog and Toad*—an allegory about life lessons—to a girl who will never get the chance to apply them.

OLIVER JAMES (class of 2009), after a
gap year, enrolled in Wesleyan University,
where he is majoring in biology.

If a field guide to the birds of Berkeley High School were in print, six
birds would be described as common: Rock Dove (City Pigeon), House
Sparrow, House Finch, American Robin, American Goldfinch, and the
California Gull. Circulating amongst the 3,500 resident mammals, it is
possible to quickly locate all six. A pause in the courtyard often yields No.
7 (Mourning Dove), and the parched community garden has a history
of revealing the elusive eighth (Anna's Hummingbird). Unofficially, the
highest number of different bird species tallied over the course of a five-
minute passing period at Berkeley High School stands at nine. For the
record, my ninth bird came in the form of a White-Throated Swift between English and Theoretical Psychology on a Thursday in October. We
could not have had more divergent travel plans: the Swift was en route to
Central America and I was on en route to a lecture on Foucault.

One can watch birds virtually anywhere. One of my earliest memories is standing next to the placid waters of the Las Gallinas sewage
ponds, considering which I valued more: the sanitary state of my sneakers or a closer look at a vagrant Red-Necked Phalarope. To this day,
the bird remains paramount, and I like to think that this mantra has
taken me far. When I lead weekend fieldtrips for beginning birders, I
tell stories of my oral history project interviewing Northern California's
premiere birder; of putting my skills to work in a survey of the impacts
of an oil spill on Bay Area shorebirds; and of winning a national birding
competition in Texas. But I especially love to convey the thrill of holding a bird in the hand, feeling its rapid heartbeat, its utter aliveness, rec-
ognizing its personality, and sticking it in a pocket (an extra hand for a
busy field biologist). The Mono Lake Basin, I tell people, is just the place
for stuffing pockets full of birds.

Mono Lake, tucked in on the eastern slope of the Sierra Nevada, is a renowned haven for birds. Indeed, there is no other place where I've had so many birds in my pockets at one time: a Violet Green Swallow in my front right pocket, his sibling enjoying the dark serenity of my front left, a pugnacious Tree Swallow banished to the back right, and two Western Bluebirds in my jacket pockets. Such is the bounty that a field ornithologist reaps at Mono Lake. Yet, while avid bird enthusiasts often grade a place for its avian diversity, Mono stands apart because of the people who are drawn to it. Feeling like a walking bird sanctuary is a great sensation. Simultaneously working and playing amongst a dozen other walking bird sanctuaries is a whole other experience. In the summer of 2008, I spent six weeks running a field site for the Cornell Laboratory of Ornithology in the hills above Mono, surrounded by birds and people studying them. The typical day was simple yet exhilarating: Choose a bird in the morning, chase it until dusk, and then discuss what was learned that day over dinner with a fellow biologist.

An exemplary day at Mono Lake had us working with the California Gull. Emerging from my crouch, I would start picking up gull chicks and putting them in boxes in preparation for banding. As I distributed the birds, they struggled and instinctively regurgitate their stomach contents in an attempt to distract their assailant. As expected, breakfast consisted mostly of endemic Brine Shrimp, made evident by the pink mush trickling down my full-body poncho. However, the game we were playing rewarded the unexpected. "Ohhhh... No way! Neon green caterpillars!" a fellow researcher shouted out animatedly. We all rushed over to witness this previously undocumented breakfast item now splayed out all over her lap. Mildly squeamish but thoroughly elated, I slowly worked my way back through the sea of birds, trying to follow the deafening conversation of 35,000 breeding California Gulls. Smiling, I thought to myself: Who would have thought that gull barf could be a source of such great amusement?

Back in Berkeley, I am still surrounded by gulls. Numbering around 25 raucous individuals, the California Gull makes the list of one of the six most common birds on the Berkeley High grounds. Having grown weary of the bland taste of their baby food, they seem quite excited to have taken up their new jobs as the campus janitors; the diet of a high school student must seem exotic after months of Brine Shrimp. Their janitorial duties aside, they are also efficient at impelling students to walk quickly to their next class by way of their frequent aerial defecations. As I step unflinchingly out into the courtyard, I unconsciously reach for my poncho and hustle on to class.

Oscar Rojas-Soto (class of 2004) attended UC Berkeley and now runs his own company, contracting with public works agencies all over the Bay Area.

My father came to the United States in 1990, and later brought my family to the United States in 1991 when I was 3, my brother 1, and my sister a newborn. We came to this country in order to establish a better life, and in many ways, I can honestly say this country has offered my family many opportunities, even though my parents' "American Dream" did not turn out exactly as they had planned.

When we arrived, my parents struggled to find employment that would pay a decent wage. While my parents were seeking stable and adequate jobs, my family moved from place to place and stayed with family and friends. Finally, when I was 8, we were able to find a two-bedroom house of our own. Our home was in one of the roughest neighborhoods of East Oakland, where there are drug dealers just around the corner, where three of my bikes were stolen, and where my uncle and some family friends were assaulted in broad daylight. As ironic as it sounds, it was nice to find a place that we could call our own.

Although our housing situation stabilized, our economic situation soon took a downturn when my dad's health worsened due to a work accident he had a couple of years earlier that injured his back. After having a couple of operations, he developed rheumatoid arthritis. This left him unable to work, and it was up to my mother to find a job that would support the household. The constant stress of working, while still trying to manage a household and take care of my father, slowly began to take a toll on my mother's emotional health. She always looked tired and overworked, so I tried to help her as much as I could by taking care of my younger siblings. As the years passed, she became more and more emotionally unstable and constantly felt depressed. Once I was in high school, I remember neither parent was able to work at a steady job.

Eventually, after finding it impossible to make ends meet, my parents decided it would be best to return to Mexico. My siblings and I were confused; we didn't know where we fell into their plan. We could not imagine having to leave all of our friends and go live in a country we hardly knew. Knowing that it would be hard for us to make a transition to life in Mexico, and still wanting at least the children to take advantage of the opportunities in the United States, my parents told us that my siblings and I would stay in the United States with another family, while my parents would go back to Mexico.

By late 2001, my parents had already left for Mexico, and my siblings and I were under the care of Luis and Carmen Baez. We were devastated by the sudden separation of our family, however our legal guardians were very supportive, and stimulated us to do well in school, even though neither of them had had the opportunity to finish high school. It was during this period of my life that I really became interested in religion. Carmen and Luis encouraged us to read and study the Bible, which came to be a consolation and aid to us in overcoming the sadness of being separated from our parents. Another way that I dealt with the situation was by succeeding academically. I became very active in school and concentrated on my work in order to keep my mind busy and to help deal with the hardship of not having my parents close to me.

Another way that I dealt with these issues was by becoming very involved in the community around me. I joined several clubs and organizations, such as TOJIL, Kids Care International, and La Raza Unida. I realize how, even though I had gone through a lot in my life, there were still other underprivileged youth who had gone through worse obstacles in life than me. And I wanted to help them do well in life, either by keeping them off the streets and doing positive activities, or by educating them about their ancestral roots and their history.

I was officially adopted in March of 2003. Only three months later, my step-dad died of a heart attack. This also was a tough period of my life; I dealt with this by keeping myself busy with schoolwork, and working to help out my family economically. If I had the opportunity to attend a University of California, I could become better prepared to help those around me and in my community to also do well in life.

RACHEL ORKIN-RAMEY (class of 1997) graduated from Amherst College in 2001 and is business director for Christie's department of Asian art in Manhattan.

Connie Pearlstein always reminded me of a big, dark crow, swooping across the yard or the classroom. When you're 5 years old, the details dominate the picture, so I have an interesting slant on what I remember of my kindergarten teacher from that year. Connie (everyone called her Connie) had a deep, booming voice, heavy black eyebrows, and she stood a mile high. She always wore wool. These are the physical characteristics that I remember: tall and wool. The wool part is important—she always wore wool pants, long wool sweaters that she had knitted, and big coats that flapped around her. She was imposing, but we adored her.

I'm not sure why the others loved her, but I loved her because she made me feel important. She talked without condescension, even if we deserved to be condescended to. Connie stood firm amid the chaos, while we hung onto her pants. All we could reach were her knees, but we wanted to hold her. When she read to us, which was anytime she could, kids held onto her like a security blanket. Connie loved books fiercely and deeply, and so we also loved them. She would check books out of the school library, huge stacks, taller than I was, and so many that the librarian got angry. Connie is one reason why for me, many things rank a distant second to a good book.

In spite of all this, I doubt that would have influenced me as much had she not kept in touch with me. I know no other people who still talk to their kindergarten teachers. She calls several times a year, and every time, she starts by saying, "Hello, Rach, this is Connie Pearlstein." She drawls out her name, so the first syllable of "Connie" takes as much time to say as the rest of her name. She is the only person I have ever let call me "Rach," even when I was young and my full name was a mouthful. Her manner of treating me as a friend carries over to this day, when I get packages from her addressed to "Friend Rachel."

I am expecting two books of Greek and Roman plays from her. One, she said, is a little battered. She kicked it across the field at Scripps after a particularly bad day in class. She still pushes books and articles on me, although now I'm an eager recipient. She does the same thing with her grandchildren. She says, "When they get a present from Grams, they know it's a book."

When Connie taught me, she was commuting several hours from Pacific Grove to Berkeley. The five daughters she had raised by herself had grown up and left home. She retired when I was in first grade, and now she lives in Pacific Grove full time. I remember her house—warm, dark, crowded with piles of books and knitting. (Some things change, but the wool remains the same.) She said that her house was haunted. I think that if Connie had been architecture, she would have been a cottage, with books and cats and armchairs. A place I'd like to live in.

Ruby Spring (class of 2013) planned to attend the Franklin W. Olin College of Engineering in Needham, Massachusetts.

Honestly, I'm not a people person. I'm more interested in observing people socialize than in taking part myself. So I spend most of my free time in solitude, painting and drawing and playing my cello. The euphoria I feel in the moments when my mind is free and my arms and hands are moving a paintbrush over canvas or a bow across cello strings is seldom evoked by social interactions. But sometimes I pause in my solitary train of thought, my brush hovering an inch from the canvas with a new color to be laid beside the old, and I wonder, am I missing something? Do I really enjoy being alone, or am I just too selfish and lazy to try to understand other people?

One Friday afternoon in late October, I dragged five buckets of sidewalk chalk to the main courtyard of UC Berkeley. I began filling in cement tiles with colorful designs, starting at the base of a tree near the center of the courtyard. Within fifteen minutes, a group of students had crowded around. "What's this for?" one asked.

"Nothing really, it's just for fun. You're all welcome to take some chalk and fill in some squares!" I stood up and smiled at them, gesturing toward an open bucket.

"I'd love to, but I don't know what to draw…"

"Draw anything! You could even just fill in a square with one color."

The group decided to stay. For the next five hours, there was a steady flow of people, chalk, and socializing, with me at the center of it all. "Who are you?" "What is this for?" "What should I draw?" "This is so therapeutic!" and, as they left, "This was so much fun!" "Thank you so much!" It was very exciting, slightly overwhelming, and a total blast. Slowly, the crowd dwindled, until at about three in the morning I got up off my powder-covered hands and knees and looked around. There were five people left: A middle-aged man drawing a UFO, three girls writing a quote from a famous singer, and a very drunk boy in an Afro wig playing a melodica. I stepped back, taking in the immensity of the colored pavement. The artwork sprawled thirty feet outward from the tree, its chalk-dust sheen shimmering softly in the moonlight. Each design was at once connected to and separate from the whole, each perspective and vision unique yet harmonious. I saw the importance of each design did not exist in its separation from the others, but in its coexistence with them. This artwork did not belong to me alone, but to the man drawing the UFO, the three girls, the musician, the participating community.

When I'm alone I can focus on myself in ways I otherwise would not. But my solitude is selfish if I don't take what it teaches me and turn it into something that stands not separate from, but part of, the world we all share.

SARAH TRUE (class of 2007) graduated from Barnard College in 2011 and works with the National Council on Crime and Delinquency in Oakland.

I step onto the hard dirt road. A warm breeze from Lake Victoria blows my hair across my grinning face. My hands smell of paint. My group and I arrived in Africa after four months of intense fund-raising and have just finished painting a mural on the walls of the hospital in Shirati, Tanzania. Turning from a large dirt road with potholes the size of elephants onto a small dirt path with potholes the size of mere warthogs, I start the walk home. I pass clay, thatch-roofed huts and nonchalantly step over a rope connecting the horns of a bull to a bush. It is my fourth week in Shirati, and avoiding roaming cows, goats, and chickens has become second nature. As I pass Mama Baraka's house of fifteen orphans, I pause and scan for my favorite little girl, the girl who has a piece of my heart. I don't see her and walk on with my shoulders slumped. But sure enough, an ecstatic smile stretches across my face when the familiar footsteps pitter-patter on the path behind me. I turn to see Nema racing towards me, barefoot, clumsily ignoring the rocks and holes, running with as much grace as a 4-year-old can.

As she dashes towards me, I question why I get a roof over my head, running water, a bed, and health care, why I get a free education and complain about homework, when Nema may never set foot in a classroom. Because I came to Shirati to teach kids about HIV, it's ironic that this little girl, orphaned by AIDS, is teaching me so much about life. Spending time with her every day brings home to me the dismal conditions that my friends here experience daily. Nema makes me realize that although it is just one month and just one child, doing what I can to make this one child feel special is making a difference. She makes me realize that I am taking small steps to make a life valued. As I will pursue a career in international public health, these steps will continue to a place where I can influence people to treat a deprived African child not just as a sad statistic, but as a girl who is as important as I am. In doing this, I hope that I can leave Nema with more than a piece of my heart and a new pair of shoes.

Now I see that my smile is mirrored on her face, and the shine in her eye, I know, is mirrored in mine. A few feet away she takes her final leap into my arms, and I pull her into an embrace and begin to tickle her, just to hear her soft, seldom-heard laugh. As always, I lose myself in this moment, when we can forget our troubles, that she is one of fifteen orphans of AIDS, she doesn't own a pair of shoes, she can't go to school because she can't afford a uniform, and she may not have eaten today. When I swing her around, we know that even for this short amount of time, we are special to each other.

SASCHA ATKINS-LORIA (class of 2004) graduated from Vassar College and is working on a master's in social work at Smith College. She is currently on placement in San Francisco working with adults on welfare. Common Ground, the program she joined sophomore year at BHS, no longer exists.

"My aunty and my mama don't like white people," Patrice tells me. Hot air blows through the windows of our freshman English classroom, and my skin burns. Patrice keeps talking. "Me, I like white people. They cool." I look up at her quickly and she laughs loudly to disguise her discomfort. Am I nothing but another white face, my flaws and quirks irrelevant because of my color? I blink quickly to lock the stinging frustration inside my eyes.

"Did you ever think that all white people aren't the same?" I ask her slowly. Patrice shrugs, looks down at her own dark skin, and then pulls out an assignment we are working on together.

"Go ahead, work," she orders. The bell rings as I glare at the paper she points to, and I push my way through too many desks out into a mess of people stumbling down the hallway.

I don't blame Patrice; it was her attempt to compensate for the prejudice of her family that led her to tell me she likes "white people." It is not my place to be angry, and Patrice's comment is what I must accept as a result of the tears her aunty and mama must have shed. Their tears are not my fault, but they have become mine to carry, and I know I shouldn't complain about the load.

At the end of freshman year, I decide to join Common Ground, a diverse program focusing on environmental and social change. However painful and heavy others' tears are to carry, I would rather bear that weight than join the mostly white, upper-middle class students as they separate themselves from the diversity of Berkeley High into the AP track. I am taking hard classes of a different sort, because I believe there is much to learn through experience.

* * *

It is sophomore year, and we sit in a Common Ground U.S. history class. Pictures of President Hoover slide across a TV screen, while a group of African-American students talk loudly in the back of the room. The movie is shut off abruptly, but it is hardly noticeable as the noise of the class escalates.

"Please stop talking." The voice of the teacher is lost to laughter. "I will not accept this. Silence!" One girl in the back finally takes notice, and she turns around.

"I don't have to listen to you," she tells the teacher loudly.

"I am your teacher."

"I don't give a damn if you are my teacher."

"I already learned this. This is for your benefit. I already went to college, I don't know if you ever will." Now we are silent, and we wait to see how far he will go. He is a teacher not made for kids who bear the weight of their family's tears, who cannot listen to stories of white men who didn't need to cry. The girl stops, she didn't expect this, but she isn't surprised.

"At least I ain't fat." She has nothing left to insult, she has been stripped of all power. She struggles to keep her face hard after another white man has reminded her of her insignificance. I hang my head as my teacher orders her out of the room.

The year ends, and I am left with moments such as these burning my memory, and little new knowledge of history or English. I cannot hold it all any more, and now I am not sure the sacrifice of a conventional education is worth it. I cannot bear another year of watching teachers attempt and fail to reach out to kids who never learned how to be students in this educational system. Midway through high school, I have not yet heard a passionate teacher discuss a book. I'd like to have that experience, and the only way to get the one "good" English teacher for junior year is to join another program called Academic Choice.

* * *

My English teacher sets his copy of *Stranger in the Village* by James Baldwin on his desk, and looks down at the cramped rows of mostly white faces below him.

"I guess we can relate this story to ourselves," he tells us. I look around the room at the eighteen Academic Choice kids with whom I spend most of my day. Many look up uneasily, waiting for our teacher to continue. We hope our too quiet silence doesn't betray our discomfort. This teacher, however, expects such respect and attention because, as he often points out, we chose to be here.

"Well, look around," he says. Then I notice that out of the five kids of color who ended up in this class by default of the computer, only one has shown up today. "Dennis?" he questions. Everyone now focuses on the one black kid, and I find myself waiting, defensively. "You are in a similar situation to the author of *Stranger in the Village.* How does it feel to be the only African American student in class?"

Dennis doesn't look around, hardly looks up, and responds quickly, "Fine."

"But do you ever feel uncomfortable? Is it hard for you?"

"It's fine." Dennis keeps his face flat, his hands on his desk, and I ache to change the subject. The too-quiet silence has intensified. I try to imagine staring out from Dennis' eyes onto a blur of well-intentioned white faces, and I watch my teacher intently, trying to decide if he realizes his mistake. I never expected such an intelligent and experienced teacher to cross this line, and I struggle to convince myself that he will never cause such humiliation again. We settle back into our normal attentive silence, and I attempt to concentrate on the story, and not on the reminder of what I have given up by joining this program.

I cannot seem to find the right balance between demanding academics and a broader education, and for the moment, I have stopped searching for it in my classes. I sometimes think I have taken the easier way out. I have chosen hours of homework, high expectations, and no exceptions. Behind me, for now, I leave the work that so far has been too hard to finish, work that I must someday return to—to help dry history's tears from Patrice's face, and to sit in a class full of color, a rainbow of engaged students.

SAM LYON (class of 2007) graduated from UC San Diego and is working in Washington, D.C. at a design and architecture company.

I have always liked problem-solving. The idea that numbers indicate how fast to thrust a jet or how powerfully to shock a spastic heart to restore it to its natural rhythm fascinates me. Last year, however, I discovered that math problems are broader than numbers, they encompass motivation and understanding as well.

My sophomore year, I had an inexperienced math teacher. I almost never rely on, or even use, the textbook for a class, because I find textbooks more confusing and less interesting than teachers. This time, however, I was forced to decipher the strange examples and pictures in my textbook to glean the formulas I needed. The book put up a fight, but failed to prove itself worse than my teacher.

Junior year, to my dismay, I discovered that a good friend of mine had the same textbook. Since we often did our homework together, I attempted to explain the book to him. Teaching my friend forced me to assume a different perspective: Instead of just trying to figure out how I could solve a given problem, I had to figure out a way to show him how to solve it. I realized very quickly that my friend just did not see the symphony of numbers I saw when I solved a problem. My solution was to give my friend the tools and step back. Instead of forcing him to approach math problems the same way I did, I merely substituted my own drawings for confusing ones in the textbook, and gave the concept explanations the textbook lacked altogether. With this boost, my friend began doing problems successfully his own way.

That same year I learned that math problems not only could include understanding but motivation as well. In my junior year, I helped create Partnerships for Success, a Berkeley High program that pairs students in remedial or otherwise decelerated math classes with students in advanced math courses for a year-long tutoring partnership. I worked with a sophomore geometry student. Initially, I assumed her bad grades meant she didn't care about school. I braced myself for a year of conflicting values and low effort. However, it took me little time to realize that she did care. She was cheerful, interested in the material, and never seemed reluctant when we were scheduling our next session. I couldn't understand why she was failing geometry.

Abruptly one day, she informed me that her friends thought she should drop out of school. They had pointed to her low grades and essentially asked her: Why bother? For me, raised to eat, sleep, and drink college, hearing this was dumbfounding. From that point on, my tutoring role became two-pronged: math and motivation.

Every Tuesday and Thursday, we met in our math classroom for an hour. She often said, "I'm so stupid!" whenever she made a mistake, no matter how small. One day I stopped her mid-phrase, looked straight into her eyes, and said, "Don't say that. Both of us know you're smart." She looked at me for what felt like a very long moment, during which I'm sure my cheeks turned red, before nodding and returning her eyes to her paper, scanning for her error. As the year progressed, so did her grades. Finally, in May, she showed me a B-plus she'd earned on a unit test. The grade reflected her hard work, but I felt as if maybe a very, very small slice of the cake had my name written on it.

SAM SHAW (class of 2010)
is attending the University of Pennsylvania.

A Barbie lies comfortably in the deep pocket of a baseball glove; a herd of plastic horses stands motionless in the middle of the floor, staring down a knotted pile of jeans and T-shirts resting in the corner. Above is one bunk, concealed in flowery quilts, stuffed dogs, and puffy pillows of all colors, accompanied by a shelf with ceramic animals, a diary, and a Disneyland snow globe. Below is another bunk, covered with everything from sweatshirts to textbooks. It is chaotic, it is colorful, it is our room.

I have shared a room with my little sister, Rosie, for most of my life. Our communal space reflects our relationship: We are very different, yet we function together harmoniously. We live in cramped quarters; we are in a constant state of wordless negotiation. It has become habit for me to knock on my own closed bedroom door before entering. I tread lightly at night, so as not to wake the slumbering creature up above. There is no space in my house that I can truly call my own. As a result, I'm closer to my sister than anyone else. While my friends argue ferociously with their younger siblings, Rosie and I joke and play-wrestle. Those who do not know us well are taken aback by our closeness. We laugh constantly. We tease each other mercilessly. We've spent hours scouring for crabs under moss-covered rocks on vacation, watching *Mythbusters* together, playing a finger game we call Chopsticks, and inventing ridiculous songs about each other.

Several years ago, my parents planned a home remodel in which Rosie and I each would get our own rooms. I thrilled at the prospect of inviting friends into my own personal space, with only my own possessions. I pestered my parents about it daily, appointing myself as the architect, contractor, and interior decorator, declaring all of my fickle plans, from the color scheme to the arrangement of the furniture, to where I would keep my old *Star Wars* action figures. However, just as we were about to finalize the plans, my dad lost his job, and the project was put on hold—indefinitely.

For years, I wanted so much to have what my friends had: a personal haven, a retreat, a sanctuary. Now, having endured living in the same room with my sister for eleven years, I realize what a gift it has been to me. Some say that those who live in tight quarters get along well with others. And I do. I pride myself on being a kind, respectful, honest person. Rosie has taught me this. Spending so much time with someone six years my junior has taught me patience and poise in my summer camp counseling jobs over the years. As a rower for my high school crew team, I have realized that the pull and sweep of the oar in synchronization with my teammates is not unlike role-modeling for her through example. Her determination to better herself at trumpet has compelled me to appreciate my musical friends in their endeavors. The hours I have spent helping her with her homework have encouraged me to seek help for myself.

I am thankful that I never had my own room. I believe I'm a better person because of the plastic horses underfoot and the hulking pink Pegasus perched on the bunk overhead. Despite my sister's occasional pesky behavior, I know she has helped me in more ways than not. Last June, at her fifth-grade graduation, Rosie and her classmates each announced their personal heroes. Rosie chose me. For a moment, I was right up there with Barack Obama, LeBron James, J.K. Rowling, Amelia Earhart, Jackie Robinson, and Spiderman. The gratitude goes both ways. Virginia Woolf once insisted on a room of one's own. I, however, will be always grateful to Rosie for what she has taught me in a room of our own.

SKYLAR JAMES (class of 2006) graduated from UC Santa Cruz in 2010 with a degree in modern literature, and is now living in the Bay Area working both as an Emergency Medical Technician and a bartender.

Growing up was tough on my relationship with my father. He is a film-maker, and worked late hours in San Francisco editing movies. In fact, the only time we really talked was when he would abandon his equipment to have a nice sit-down dinner with the family. And even then, the attention was shared between my mother and brother. But what I would always truly desire would be for him to tell me one of his world-famous stories. In those ten, maybe fifteen, minutes, all was right in the world. In those short moments, nothing was wrong in our relationship. But these stories were only rare treats, in an otherwise bland relationship.

One night last summer, however, my father invited me to San Francisco to turn off some equipment. "So there I was, escaping from the burning barracks with the rest of my platoon," he said, with such fire in his lungs it startled me. "We had been hit in the middle of the night. One minute I was dreaming about canned peaches and sauce, the next, guys are screaming." He took a moment to read an advancing sign on the free-way. "It wasn't until I had made it out that I realized we were missing a man. Not just any man, no, no, no, we were missing our sergeant!"

I was instantly intrigued. My Dad was delivering the story in such a way that it felt as if I were right next to him in Vietnam.

"'Where's Sergeant Jones?' I asked a nearby soldier. They said he was in the burning house, still sleeping. When I asked why they didn't wake him, you know what they said?" he asked me. I shook my head. "They said," he continued, "that he was a nigger, and they wouldn't stick their neck out for any nigger." My eyes opened a little wider at this remark. It had always been an unwritten rule in my family to never say "nigger."

"So I said, 'Hey! I'm a nigger, would you leave me?' None of those boys responded, which answered my question."

"So what happened next?" I asked. My Dad just smiled briefly and glanced at me before saying, "I went into that barracks and dragged our sergeant out." He had said it so quickly I could not tell if he would elaborate. A few seconds went by before I asked him what I thought was an obvious question. "So … did you get a medal or something?"

"No," he replied. The fiery talk had vanished from his lips, and the excitement in his face turned to a calm, bitter expression. He sighed, "Sergeant Jones never reported what happened that night. In fact he gave me the worst possible grunt work."

I was thoroughly confused. "Wow, I guess it wasn't worth it, then," I blurted out. The car made a sudden turn to the side of the street we were now on, and came to a stop. The lights of passing cars danced off our faces. It was so quiet I almost could hear our heartbeats thumping; mine in anticipation, his in preparation.

He turned to me and said, "Son, sometimes doing the right thing doesn't mean you get a trophy or recognition. Sometimes, doing the right thing just means you can sleep easier at night." The silence was reinstated. After a few minutes he gave me a pat on the shoulder, and a passing car's lights revealed his smile. My Dad turned on the motor back on, and we pulled back onto the street.

My father's stories have influenced me in two significant ways. First, he showed me that doing something good or brave shouldn't be solely for recognition. It should be about what is right, and how it can help others rather than just oneself. Secondly, he showed me why I want to become a writer—to share my stories and lessons, and perhaps help someone else sleep easy at night.

SONIA ABRAMS (class of 1999) graduated in 2003 from Lewis and Clark College and is working in the Bay Area as a speech language pathologist.

It's 6 a.m. on a cool July morning in Taylorsville, California, a town that's only four blocks long. The rickety barn creaks above my head as I stand ankle-deep in horse manure, brushing the knots out of my favorite horse's mane. My friends back home in the city are curled up warm in their beds. They wonder why every summer I go to a place where I have to get up at the crack of dawn and wear muddy clothes to be a ranch hand. But I know why. I do it to feel the wet nose of a horse as it nuzzles my arm, begging for a treat. I do it because of the way I laugh as I try to keep up with the fast-paced line dancing, and for the screams of excitement as the cowboy hangs on to the bull for dear life.

As I scoop horse dung, I stop to think of the day ahead of me. I've been working on a running ranch for two weeks, and today it's coming to an end. In just a couple of hours, I'll be in a van with other muddy campers on our way back to the real world. I had gone to camp expecting to make some friends and enjoy typical camp recreation. But working in such an intense environment, close to animals, I soon discovered the commitment it takes to care for cows, horses, goats, and pigs. As a small girl, I was always digging up salamanders in the garden, running to pet new dogs tied up outside stores, and trying to identify a bug we recently captured in the backyard. My work on the ranch made my real interests come alive.

I live in Berkeley, California, a city known as one of the most diverse and bizarre places in the country. People in Berkeley are accepting of everything: races, cultures, sexualities, clothing, music. My closest friends listen to almost every kind of music: rap, hip-hop, swing, salsa, ska, alternative, and reggae.

So when I came home from living on a ranch with a passion for country music and ranch animals, I assumed my friends would be open to the new culture. Little did I realize that Berkeley is not the place for country bumpkins. Berkeley may have a lot of great crazes, but boot stomping, bull riding, and stall mucking aren't among them. These are the essential ingredients that make up what I love in country life.

All my life, country music has been a big influence. I was 7 years old when I decided to play the violin. Instead of playing classical music, like most other young violin players, I was drawn to bluegrass and klezmer. I loved how quick it was and how my fingers flew across the strings like they were dancing. At first, I played small gatherings and little coffee houses. At age 12, my group performed in front of 1,600 people. It made me happy to see people clapping, smiling, and dancing to the music. Most people don't realize that violin and fiddle are actually the same instrument. My friends try to picture me with a violin. They think of old men in tuxedos and powdered wigs playing Bach in front of stuffy old women. On the contrary, bluegrass music is jumping and dancing, people hooting and hollering from the audience.

I've tried to convince my city friends to give country music a try, but it's no use. However, my attempts have produced some surprising reactions. Recently, I was driving with a friend of mine, and I had the radio tuned to the one country station you can pick up in Berkeley. He refused to even listen, and without any warning tried to jump out of my car! Country lifestyle is one thing I'm on my own about. I have to listen to country in my bedroom and go to the rodeo with only my camp friends. By discovering my friends' closed-mindedness, I have learned a lot about myself. I never thought of giving up my taste for something different, so I had to learn how to branch out and pursue my own passion. This has influenced my academic interests as well. My interest in biology and my decision to pursue a pre-veterinary program have been my own. The colleges I am applying to are determined by this passion and not by where my friends plan to go. I also have a new respect for the myriad directions my friends are choosing. I've learned that although it can be awkward and lonely to cut out on my own, it is worth it. I don't have to conform to what everyone else likes, so I'm free to show my individuality. I can learn more about who I am and who other people are. Now, it's fun to have something unique: something only I appreciate. I realize this is where open-mindedness begins.

TARYN RIEMER (class of 2011)
is a student at Brown University.

It was 10:30 on a warm summer night, and I was trapped in the sewing room—or, more specifically, I was in the sewing room trapped under a half-finished tissue paper monstrosity. I had only been in the four-week fashion design program at the California College of the Arts for a few days, and after a whirlwind of classes in drawing, clothing construction, and the ins and outs of the fashion industry, we had been assigned our first major challenge: create an avant-garde gown illustrating our design aesthetic, using only pink tissue paper and pins. Well, knowing my aesthetic was easy. Ever since the age of 5, when I had first broken into my mother's collection of scarves and draped them into a Grecian gown, I had understood my own style. While I'd matured over the next twelve years, I still found beauty in a bolt of softly sweeping chiffon or in the hint of a silk slip peeking out from under a skirt. No, the problem here was easing the ideas out of my head, through my fingertips, and into the rapidly growing pile of tissue paper that sat half-heartedly tacked to my dress form. The purpose of the project was, after all, to work outside our technical construction ability—while I couldn't sew the dress from tulle or velvet, I could see my wildest visions come to life in a 3-D form. The project was undeniably daunting.

I have been sewing since I was 10, when I begged my neighbor to let me borrow her creaky sewing machine, which hadn't seen the outside of a basement since before I was born. After lugging the heavy box across the street, I plopped down on my bed to devour the instruction manual, trying out each step as I read. It took several tries for my clumsy fingers to thread the needle, but once I had conquered the tiny eye of the needle I was ready to start sewing. My first few seams were ragged, unsightly lines that cut through the scrap of cotton like poorly paved roads. I just kept sewing, though—stitch after stitch, seam after seam. Despite my poor first attempts, I was a fast learner. I was soon sewing simple projects, then more complicated ones, until I eventually began to sew garments.

As I worked away at the sewing machine over the years, I slowly discovered a culture I had never before encountered—the world of fashion history. I was entranced by the classic, feminine lines of vintage pieces and feasted on the fashion section at the public library, where I would find books on the styles of every past decade. Soon, instead of buying patterns from the local fabric store, I was spending hours sifting through piles of old patterns at yard sales or antique stores for the perfect 1940s shirtwaist dress. I began to frequent vintage fairs, fingering a silky beaded shift from the 1920s or a full cotton skirt from the 1950s, waiting for the magical moment when—ah, yes—my fingers landed upon the piece I had been searching for. It was pure joy when I discovered a fuchsia veiled headband or a pair of tiny flowered court shoes seemingly plucked straight off Audrey Hepburn's feet. My love of vintage led me through the pages of my grandmother's photo albums, through stacks of fashion history books, between stalls at antique fairs, and finally back to where it all began: my beloved sewing machine, where I brought my passion to life in the form of a tea-length 1948 summer dress. The simple cotton dress, with frothy sea foam green flowers, was my first vintage success.

My love of fashion continued to expand during my junior year, when I founded and led a fashion club in which students could share their enthusiasm for design. The club produced a fashion magazine featuring vintage pieces altered in order to modernize them. We carried out the idea with a staff of student designers, stylists, makeup artists, photographers, and models. We shot the six-page color spread and then complemented it with articles about the ethics of the fashion industry, editorial pages on the latest trends, and designs from our own club members. Through our combined efforts, the magazine was a great success.

All of these experiences led me to the moment when, back at the workroom, I began to craft paper into complicated frames I had only read about in costume history books and never dreamed of being able to create myself. Several attempts later, I finally settled on a contraption modeled after an eighteenth-century frame called a pannier. After finding success in my first prototype, I soon completed several billowing pillows of tissue that, when secured under the dress, gave the skirt seemingly effortless volume. While the gown I made was only out of pink tissue paper, I know that I will some day be sewing in velvet.

TING W. HUNG (class of 2002)
attended UC San Diego.

My father and I once again stood at the arrival lounge at the airport on a hot summer night, waiting for my mother's arrival from Hong Kong. It would have been six months since we last saw her at the departure end of the same airport. This would be one of her two visits to us this year, her second visit would be in the Christmas time during her winter vacation. Her visit this time would be about three weeks, as usual in her past visits to us, then she would have to go back to her career as a violinist in Hong Kong. Since my father and I moved to the United States six years ago from Hong Kong, my mother and I have been living in two separate worlds that are bridged by long-distance calls and her regular visits to the United States.

The exit doors swung open, and passengers began flooding out of customs, many of them searching very anxiously for their loved ones and hugging them out of overflow of emotion. But my father and I, we were very casual. After all, we had been to the lounge so many times to pick up my mother that all this had become routine. I stood very calmly; I felt no thrill seeing my mother at that moment, even though we had not seen each other in such a long time. Maybe it was because we have not lived together in such a long time that my impression of her had slowly faded. Then, she came out of the exit; we approached her, carried her luggage, and drove home.

For three weeks, she stays and lives with us in the apartment that for most of the year is occupied only by my father and me. The first few days of her visits are often the hardest time to live through, the transition from the absence of someone very close to the immediate presence of that someone returning into my life. I live so independently on my own when my mother is away, even though we stay connected weekly through the phone, I always feel distant to her when she comes because of the time missing in our relationship. The gap between us always takes some time to shorten. But once I have adjusted to the addition to our life, I'd find my mother once again is "my mother." Despite my permanent relationship with my father, there are holes within me that only my mother can fill. She offers me help and advice about school and other decisions, and I passionately accept her help. Whenever I'm stressed out about schoolwork, especially in the subject of English and writing, she is the first that I go to, even though she can't even understand English. I go to her because she offers me encouragement and motivation. She was the one who talked me into trying out for sports, encouraging me to go for badminton because it fit into our Chinese cultural heritage. Gradually, we forget all our differences, and we live as if we've never been separated. I feel motivated just by her presence, knowing that there's someone supporting me. All her words have made me a healthier person, both physically and mentally: My schoolwork improves, I'm more attentive and interested in a lot of different activities, and I'd feel very positive about almost anything.

Time goes by very fast, the three weeks are up and back to the airport where it began. She goes back to her life and we go on with our own, my father and I. We know that she'll be back in the winter time, but for me, it gets to be very difficult to handle the adjustment within; from living so independently from my mother for most of the time, to feeling her existence in my life and then going back to living without her presence. The long-distance relationships between us, and all the toss-up of feelings that I have, are hard to go through once every six months. The contrast between loneliness and hardship, encouragement and love, shape and reshape my character. Having all these experiences has made my values grow stronger and more mature: I grow more upon every one of her visits, and I am influenced by her words even after her departure. Every time I watch her go away at the airport, I always remind myself about all her encouragement and advice that will stay, even though physically an ocean separates us.

WHITNEY SMITH (class of 1997) graduated from Brown University in 2001 and from UC Davis School of Medicine in 2008. She is practicing psychiatry in the Bay Area.

Short but mighty women have a long tradition in my family. At five foot two, I am eye-level with the two impressive women who are my grandmothers. Despite their common height, they are as different as can be. From them I inherit not only my size, but the personality to back it up.

My maternal grandmother uses whatever tool she has on hand to accomplish the task before her; she has been known to butter bread with a butcher knife. She moved to Brazil when she was 29. She had never left the United States before, didn't speak a word of Portuguese, and had two small children. Undaunted, she threw herself into the adventure. After Brazil, she moved to Iran, visited communist Russia, and was a librarian in Papua New Guinea. (One of my Halloween costumes included a genuine grass skirt!) When she moved to California, I was 7 years old. Though finished with traveling, she did not become a conventional grandmother. With Grandma, I danced in the San Francisco Carnaval Parade (she loved it) and passed through the portals of Victoria's Secret for the first time. (She put down her foot at the purple satin bra—"What would your father say?") The importance of a well-fitting white shirt and a good book are among her legacies to me.

Mummers, my father's mother, has lived on the same street, just two blocks from her parents' home, since she married the boy next door more than sixty years ago. I live just around the corner and visit her often. She has taught me many things: to embroider, to stew spiced cherries, and, most important, to listen. A visit to Mummers never fails to include sitting at her kitchen table with a plate of gingersnaps. I've watched her put visitors at ease with well-worded questions designed to draw out personal interests. She is a traditionalist who appreciates orderliness but is not rigid in her thinking. She truly learns from the people around her, and they love her for it. She is willing to always listen to me, but I have discovered that it is I who can learn from her. Whether the subject be my friends, her childhood, the National Organization for Women, or religion, her insight and knowledge have helped me form my own opinions. In addition to all of her grace, she has, at 82, conquered Windows 95 and e-mail.

As I've grown older, I've discovered that aspects of my two grandmothers' personalities are fused in me. Like Grandma, I throw my entire self into whatever activity lies at hand. Sophomore year, I became the managing editor of the school paper. My job description was summed up in two sentences by the editor in chief. "You make sure the advertisements make it into the paper and call the printer. I don't really know what else you do." Left on my own, I looked around to see where I could be helpful. Two years later, my job has expanded to include a multitude of tasks. I spend so many hours at school that even the janitors say hi to me. I am in charge of printing, circulation, and advertising. I attend PTSA meetings, Back to School Night, and eighth-grade outreach events to expose parents to the paper. I write thank you letters for donations and telephone patrons not receiving the paper. I run the business staff. Like Mummers, I listen to other people and help when I can. When an editor's page is lost on the computer, I comfort and help them. When a writer is having trouble with a story, I help them find someone to interview. Although I am now a veteran on the paper, I never stop listening to others, incorporating their ideas and learning from them.

It is from Grandma and Mummers that I inherit my determination, cheerfulness, value of education, and, above all, love of family. I am, however, my own person. No one else laughs as hard at themselves as I do. No one else loves organizing trips to the beach in the middle of the winter. No one else would venture to Paris by themselves and return with only one souvenir—a pair of three-inch cork platform shoes (to bolster my height, of course.)

YELIZAVETA RUZER (2004) graduated from Clark University in 2008 and is working as an evaluation coordinator at a Bay Area consulting firm that helps public benefit agencies with grant writing, strategic planning, and evaluation.

My family and I waited nine years for permission to emigrate from Russia. In 1991, we were given ten days to pack our belongings and leave. We settled in Berkeley, where I was enrolled in kindergarten. On the first day, I wore shoes and clothes donated by the Jewish Family and Children's Services, including my first pair of sneakers. In Russia, my only shoes had been a pair of functional yet unremarkable boots. The sneakers were the most beautiful shoes I had ever seen, with three shades of pink and white laces. I proudly walked to my first day of school thinking that everyone would admire them. To my surprise, no one noticed. I didn't understand why all my classmates didn't crowd around me. Surely, in my old neighborhood, everyone would have. I realized that things were different in this new country.

Coming to America brought other significant changes. For the first time, my family and I were allowed to practice our religion freely. My family joined a nearby synagogue that we still attend today. I was enrolled in the synagogue's Hebrew School and attended its summer camp. The fight my parents endured to live in a country where we could practice our religion freely makes me appreciative of the opportunities and freedoms that I have today.

The religious freedom came at a cost, however. Things were very different outside of my family, and my parents worked hard to retain the Russian culture at home. I was given spelling tests and practiced reading and writing in Russian. I celebrate Russian New Year's with a tree, am able to cherish movies my parents grew up on, and can appreciate *The Catcher in the Rye* in both English and Russian. The greatest impact on my family, however, has been the financial struggle. I was jealous of my friends who spent their parents' money frivolously on clothes and makeup.

Today, I work three days a week behind the front desk at a yoga studio. I have also been baby-sitting two children since freshman year. Their mom takes night classes and is unable to drive me home because she is a single parent, so after baby-sitting I take an hour-long bus ride home. The money I make helps me pay for clothing, public transportation, and most of my food. I come home exhausted from the long day and must stay up late to finish my homework. At school, not many people realize what I am going through. Just as no one noticed my sneakers, not many people understand that I must work in order to persevere. I have come a long way from the day my family arrived in America. I am grateful for my experiences as an immigrant, and I can look back and see that my hard work has taught me a lot about the world. Starting from scratch has been both financially and emotionally hard, but the progress my family has made since our arrival proves that the work has paid off.

YONAS MEHARI (class of 2007) was an ethnic Eritrean whose family was deported from Ethiopia at the time of the civil war there, and subsequently made their way to the Bay Area via Yemen and Germany.

On Thanksgiving, 2006, Yonas, his mother, and older sister were tragically gunned down in their home as a result of a family feud. In the first draft of a longer essay, he wrote of the unspeakable horrors he had experienced by the age of 10, including the devastating loss of his father from a respiratory infection. He ended the essay on a positive note, by discussing his leadership role in creating the Ethiopian-Eritrean Student Union at Berkeley High. "Some people don't know where I come from," he wrote. "That is why I want to bring people together by starting a club for Ethiopian and Eritrean students that also includes other students, to help educate them and help them understand each other, and bring peace between them. I understand the importance of diversity. It's no longer abstract, but alive." He left this completed short essay, which he was working on with the help of essay reader Brenda Kahn:

Being an immigrant, it was hard for me to learn to speak and read in English. I did not read English in Ethiopia. In fact, I barely read even my own language, Amharic, because of the poor quality of the schools.

I have been in the Earphone Club for the last four years. The club is mostly to help English learners get into the habit of reading in English or in their native language by listening to a book on tape while following along in a book. The club taught me to love reading. Because of this positive experience, I recruited my friends into the club, which landed me in a leadership role. I was elected the vice president of the club in my sophomore year, a position I've held ever since. My responsibilities are to organize and plan meetings, e-mail people to remind them when the meetings are, and run the club when the president is absent. I also continue to recruit new members. Today, I don't really need the headphones to read, but I still go there every Wednesday to help others who are in the same situation as I was.

Acknowledgments

Thank you to Angela Price and Skyler Barton, Berkeley High's supportive and wise college counselors, who guide hundreds of students through the college process each year.

Thank you to Amy Crawford, a Berkeley High English teacher who collected and shared a number of her students' excellent essays. A thank you to three Berkeley High essay readers: Jamie Keller, Wendy Morrison, and Kathy Brown, who helped in the search for good essays, persuading seniors and recent graduates to contribute their essays to this collection. A thank you also to essay reader Tami Uecker, who provided sound second opinions, good feedback, and up-to-date information on the ever-evolving prompts.

Thank you to Evelyn Whitburn, a Bay Area graphic designer who contributed her time and expertise to lay out this book.

And, finally, a most heartfelt thank you to Vicky Elliott and Elaine Ratner, two professional editors and Berkeley High readers, without whom this third edition would not have happened.

This is the third edition of The Berkeley Book of College Essays. In order to make room for new essays, some beloved stories from the first and second editions were pulled. It was not easy to pick and choose, and I was sad to see each one go. In addition, many current students sent us their essays for consideration—many more than we could use. Though this comes last, first and foremost, I would like to thank our wonderful and generous students—those who appear in the book and those who don't. Their stories are a gift to Berkeley High School.

Janet Huseby